Made in His
Image

Made in His *Image*

A CALL TO ADVANCE THE FAITH

Dr. Kristy Cromblin, M.D.

LIFE EXPECTANCY, LLC
Copyright © 2018 by Kristy Cromblin, founder of Life Expectancy

ISBN-13: 978-0-692-19732-5

First Printing: 2019

Printed in the USA

Interior Design by Amnet

Edited by Lynn Ferguson and Michelle Tapia
Illustration by David Michael Rogers
Cover by Shamaria Designs

Gratitude

I truly thank God for seeing me fit to deliver such a message.
I thank You for sending Your Word to move forward with this
assignment. When I seemed to have run out of Words to say,
You never ceased.
Thank You.

*If you have lost hope in Christianity, or you're just not convinced,
hold on. Don't walk away just yet. There is so much more to
Him. Admittedly, many Christians have done a poor job in the
past of being models and trailblazers, but don't let that deter you
from something that is so great for you. Yes, there are many paths
to the divine. God would never leave us so limited. Yet ultimately
they all lead to one common path:
The path of enlightenment,
The brightest path that you will ever experience,
The path that took on a human embodiment,
The path referred to by many names,
The path that we call
Jesus.*

Contents

*This book was written for a popular audience and is of spiritual inclination.

About the Journey

Information for this book started flowing to me at about age 14, when I first began to sense the voice of God. There were times that I would ponder internally and with deep inquiry on certain questions in effort to seek an answer. Though two weeks later, and sometimes in the oddest of places, I would ALWAYS get an answer! The answer would be followed up with confirmation by hearing an expert say the exact same thing. It was all too indescribable and so for over a decade I told no one. I recall my first experience. As I sat on the edge of my bed pondering, I recall a sudden feeling of extreme elation. I remember thinking to myself that this must be what Heaven feels like. Nonetheless, that was the beginning of a stream of aphorisms and coined sayings. Though it has been slightly revised over the years, one of my first noted ones is "There is no greater pleasure than that which pleases the soul, and no greater displeasure than that which displeases the soul." I collected many other aphorisms thereafter. Even though I continued to have spiritual encounters with God, still I questioned His existence. I did not want to take my parents or grandparents word for it. No way. I had to know for myself. This private journey went on for 11 years. I even studied different religions and peeped in on a few religious practices. I appreciate those years because when I circled right back around I was well informed. Though I was never an atheist, the old combat expression, "There's no atheist in foxholes," became very relevant to me. Life's trials caused me to look no further. I soon became an unwavering Christian! Thankfully, through the years I kept my notes. Before giving serious thought to compiling them, in 2012, Dr. Julian Thomas spoke a prophetic Word to me that this book would be an inspiration. Because I'd regarded my notes as private and my own, it took some time, and even more spiritual urging. However, I knew that I had to eventually publish them. Now, in this compendium I have taken joy in sharing with you the product of my answered questions and "mental rioting" from the past decades. My prayer is that it delivers you as it has me.

Reading Guide

Note: While reading this book you will notice heavy use of pronoun flipping. This is where I take specific pronouns and alternate them within the same idea. It is with reason that I do this, as this style of writing is designed to speak directly to you. In fact, you are encouraged to take it personally. Some of what you read here may hurt and some may anger you. You may outright dismiss a few of the claims. No matter. You are invited to challenge the very context by which every scripture is cited. You are even urged to scrutinize any extra-scriptural statement written in this book. Undoubtedly, much of this work will nudge you and/or leave you with many questions. Fire away. If need be, read the material repeatedly and in segments. Focus only on what engages you until another section begins to pique your interest.

Diligently seek His Truth.

Introduction

"And God said, Let Us make man in Our image, after our likeness: and let them have dominion over the fish of the sea, and over the fowl of the air, and over the cattle, and over all the earth, and over every creeping thing that creepeth upon the earth. So God created man in His own image, in the image of God created He them."

GENESIS 1:26-27 KJV

T he above aforementioned scriptures are the premise of this work. To understand it is to start a new journey to understand you.

The human body is an exact representation of every natural pattern that God has created on earth. Therefore, it is a replica of the true essence of God. It is the most inclusive and yet the most complex design of all creation. Every phenomenon, every dynamic system that we observe has a pattern by which it has come to exist, and those patterns may be observed within the human body. Those very patterns are in you! You are a duplicate of every life form and every natural system known to man. How magnificent is that! The human body is all inclusive of every modality of life on earth. He then stepped it up and gave you a highly sophisticated neurological system topped with a reasoning mind. Thus, you are the most complex design of all His creations. You are the blueprint of all life, since the beginning of time. *You* are made in His image.

Every phenomenon that we observe is with reason and never just happenstance. Through the ages, and in God's timing, much has been revealed. In this book I will discuss many spiritual events as I align them with a more secular approach. All physical phenomena are to some degree secondary to a primary spiritual ordinance. Even though this book is written in a manner that provides practical intel on what God is up to, we will never know it all. We will never be able to comprehend it all, and neither is our human form designed for such. In fact, this is an area in which we must proceed with caution. I cannot emphasize it enough, we will not know it all. Though this book frequently engages in a logical approach, attempts to rationalize and intellectualize every spiritual phenomenon is an oxymoron that will only prove to impede your spiritual growth.

I will select some natural laws and systems and align them with several systems of the human body and psyche. These correlations will range from the theory of relativity, to the Pauli exclusion principle, and more. We will explore Albert Einstein and examine the ancient Greek philosophy of the Microcosm and Macrocosm, both of which provide the foundation to understanding this work and pose as the underlying persuasions of this book.

We will begin at the molecular level and magnify it unto the Greatest level. Throughout the book I refer to our Supreme Creator as He. Though *He* has many names, I reference Him as God. I do so, as it is the common tongue of my intended audience. However, it must be clearly stated that God is not limited to one name of any certain language. God has no form, and is therefore without the restrictions of speciation, gender, or nationality. Though there is no gender role to play, we will go along in order to effect commonality and vital expressions. Understanding and accepting these fundamentals will prepare you for the more complex and challenging portions of this work.

We will also bridge the gap between science and religion. As we continue we will build upon the making of man from mere chemicals to the beautiful, functional creation that we are- from the molecular to the masterpiece is a body that is designed to autocorrect. Yours is a body that is designed to maintain balance and equilibrium even in the midst of lack. It heals itself. You are designed to evolve such that you are compatible with your surroundings, assuring your survival in yet the most challenging environments. *All* patterns of life can be illustrated through this magnificent human body. By this we have come to understand its dynamics. By this we have come to understand the nature of life.

So, if you are an aspiring healthcare professional, then this will fortify your understanding of the human body. If you are battling to understand who you are, or just why you do and say the things that you do, stay tuned. There is a place just for you. So don't be surprised when what you read registers differently with you than it does with the next person in your book club. Though life circumstances may have tampered with and augmented your perception of your *truest* nature, yet you are beautifully and wonderfully made, on purpose. There is a message here to remind you of that. From this I pray that His truth whispers to you not by words alone, but via a personalized understanding that exceeds any words *ever written*.

You.

Howbeit when he, the Spirit of truth,
is come he will guide you into all truth:
for he shall not speak of himself;
but whatsoever he shall hear, that shall he speak:
and he will show you things to come.
JOHN 16:13 KJV

In the beginning was the Word, and the Word was with God, and the Word was God. The same was in the beginning with God. All things were made by Him; and without Him was not anything made that was made. In Him was life; and the life was the light of men.
— JOHN 1:1-4 KJV

CHAPTER 1

The Word

In the beginning was the Word…

The Word of God is law. It is an unwavering truth that not only revitalizes but gives life. His Word represents ever-present pure truth that has been present since the beginning of time. This truth is powerfully creative and has the means to take on any form imaginable. By that same notion, it also has the power to dismantle. Not every form of truth has been understood or welcomed by our conscious minds. The prophet Isaiah writes of one of the least popular truths: *"I form the light, and create darkness: I make peace, and create evil: I the Lord do all these things"* (Isaiah 45:7 KJV). He then writes in Chapter 55:10-11 NKJV

> *For as the rain comes down, and the snow from heaven, and do not return there, but water the earth, and make it bring forth and bud, that it may give seed to the sower and bread to the eater, so shall my Word be that goes forth*

from my mouth; It shall not return to me void, but it shall accomplish what I please, and it shall prosper in the thing for which I sent it.

Ever seen the snow fall in reverse? Neither will you witness the Word unaccomplished. Once truth is transmitted into our realm and the receiver processes the message, it is then ready to be translated for its intended use. Though we are notorious for rejecting His truth, yet will His truth effectively reach you.

For the Word of God is quick, and powerful, and sharper than any twoedged sword, piercing even to the dividing asunder of soul and spirit, and of the joints and marrow, and is a discerner of the thoughts and intents of the heart.
— HEBREWS 4:12 KJV

Seven Days. Again, it is very important to avoid intellectualizing certain aspects of scripture, but when aligned with Genesis this begs for exegesis. Yet, here is where I expect to lose the lot of you and get a call from my Mom. Let it be boldly noted that God is perfectly capable of creating all of creation in six days, multiple times over if He so chooses. However, what we have here is a relatable translation, which can be witnessed often throughout the bible. We can all agree that humans have been on various levels of biblical understanding and interpretation throughout time. This translation of Word reflects that. Again, God is completely able to create all there is and rest afterwards within any stretch of time of His choosing. Traditionally, we have come to accept this as seven days. However, the understanding of this time discrepancy has been gifted to mankind through Einstein in his Theory of Relativity. In the concept of *time dilation* he clearly explains how elapsed time, or the perception thereof, may differ between two different observers stationed a great distance apart. Nonetheless, in order for you to gain more from this work I challenge you to reimagine "seven days."

> *But, beloved, be not ignorant of this one thing,*
> *that one day is with the Lord as a thousand*
> *years, and a thousand years as one day.*
> — 2 PETER 3:8 KJV

Day 1: *And God said Let there be*
light: and there was light. And God
saw the light, that it was good…
— GENESIS 1:3-4 KJV

Light was God's first creation. It symbolizes His presence, love, goodness, and joy, just to name a few. The more light you have the more you can detect things otherwise unnoticed. Turning toward the light increases your visibility. This involves choosing Him, choosing love in seemingly the most impossible of times. Turn toward Him and you will come into the knowledge of so much more. This first creation can easily be viewed as a foundation for a higher walk with him. *Draw nigh to God and He will draw nigh to you" (James 4:8 KJV).*

Day 2: *Let there be a firmament in the midst of the waters, and let it divide the waters from the waters. And God called the firmament Heaven.*
— GENESIS 1:6;8 KJV

Note: Where there is water, there is life. So here the author of Genesis describes Heaven as something that has taken form, a firmament, to create a barrier between waters. This means that on either side of Heaven exists the very substance that is the essence of all life, water. In this passage God does not distinguish a difference in the quality or characteristics of the waters, so neither will I.

Day 3: *And God said Let the waters under the heaven be gathered together unto one place, and let the dry land appear; and it was so. And God called the dry land Earth; and the gathering together of the waters called He seas: and God saw that it was good. And God said Let the earth bring forth grass, the herb yielding seed, and the fruit tree yielding fruit after his kind, whose seed is in itself, upon the earth: and it was so.*
— GENESIS 1:9-11 KJV

Here we see that the focus is on the underside of the firmament. The first sign of life appears. One of the core requirements to be categorized as living is that a thing must be derived from another living entity. Herein lies the beginning of life begetting life. This unfailing system is operative yet today.

Day 4: *And God said Let there be lights in the firmament of the heaven to divide the day from the night; and let them be signs, and for seasons, and for days, and years: And let them be for lights in the firmament of the*

*heaven to give light upon the earth: and it
was so. And God made two great lights, the
greater light to rule the day and the lesser light
to rule the night: He made the stars also.*
— GENESIS 1:14-16 KJV

Light. The sun and moon shine their light through heaven and heaven acts as a conduit by which to transmit it. Recall that light is the first creation and can symbolize much, including a foundation for spiritual growth. This must pass through a higher plane, heaven. Then there's day and night. Day and night carry both literal and figurative meaning throughout the bible. Commonly we find where day and night signify the beginning and the end of a time period, respectively.

Day 5: *"And God said Let the waters bring
forth abundantly the moving creature that
hath life, and fowl that may fly above the earth
in the open firmament of heaven. And God
created great whales, and every living creature that moveth, which the waters brought
forth abundantly, after their kind, and every
winged fowl after his kind: and God saw that
it was good. And God blessed them, saying Be*

fruitful, and multiply, and fill the waters in
the seas, and let fowl multiply in the earth."
— GENESIS 1:20-22 KJV

Here we witness the first sign of lifeforms advancing, i.e. evolution. From the seedlings of Day 3, to the winged fowl mentioned above we can find identical arrangements of genetic codons. This is neither the beginning or the end of such an observation. In fact, we share a notable percent of the human genome, or complete set of DNA, with the least complex forms of life. What constitutes the least complex life forms may also be found within the most complex.

Day 6: *And God said Let the earth bring forth*
the living creature after his kind, cattle, and
creeping thing, and beast of the earth after his
kind: and it was so. And God made the beast of
the earth after his kind, and the cattle after their
kind, and every thing that creepeth upon the earth
after his kind: and God saw that it was good.
And God said Let us make man in our image,
after our likeness: and let them have dominion
over the fish of the sea, and over the fowl of the
air, and over the cattle and over all the earth and

over every creeping thing that creepeth upon the earth. **So God created man in His own image, in the image of God created He him; male and female created He them.** *And God blessed them, and God said unto them, Be fruitful and multiply, and replenish the earth, and subdue it: and have dominion over the fowl of the air, and over every living thing that moveth upon the earth. And God said, Behold I have given you every herb bearing seed, which is upon the face of the earth, and every tree, in the which is the fruit of a tree yielding seed; to you it shall be for meat. And to every beast of the earth, and to every fowl of the air, and to every thing that creepeth upon the earth, wherein there is life, I have given every green herb for meat: and it was so. And God saw every thing that He had made, and, behold, it was very good... Thus the heavens and the earth were finished, and all the host of them.*

— GENESIS 1:24-31; GENESIS 2:1 KJV

This was by far God's busiest moment of creation here on earth. He invested most of His time during this period. Not surprising, as we see the greatest evolvement of life during this period. Here we witness life advancing out of water as every land creature and its mate is created, including man.

Day 7: *And on the seventh day God ended his work which He had made: and He rested on the seventh day from all His work which He had made.*
— GENESIS 2:2 KJV

Having set all operations and mechanics in place by the end of the 6th day, He rested. There was nothing more that needed to be done, and we have been in full operation ever since. There have been provisions already made for anything that you could possibly ask.

An important comparison can be made here. On the seventh day God rested after having labored for six. In Mark 2:27, Jesus supports David's statement that the sabbath was made for man and not man for the sabbath. To further develop understanding, it must be stated that the sabbath is *not* a certain day. Specifically speaking, the sabbath is not Saturday and it is not Sunday. The sabbath however, is a crucial day that we are encouraged to set aside in order to replenish our mind, body, and soul. In biblical times, depending on the religious sect, this day was socially accepted to be either Saturday or Sunday. In fact, it was the law. The sabbath was regarded as a day of devotion to God and nothing more, and by many accounts it still is. This is not to say that you should forsake worship service by any means. In fact, Hebrews 10:25 states that we should not forsake the assembling of ourselves together and that we should encourage one another.

Contemporarily speaking, the traditional sabbath can be quite laborious for those highly active in ministry. It may serve leaders to be mindful of this for yourselves as well as your entrusted few. Nonetheless, a 24-hour period of self enhancement out of a 168-hour week is very important. It may be personalized and carried out in what way seems best for your soul. Ah, but what better way than to be assembled with kindred spirits who seek to encourage and be reminded of the teachings of Jesus Christ.

The sabbath is clearly set aside for you to replenish, rest, or do things with pure enjoyment. *Against such there is no law.* It is my professional opinion that much of what we see in healthcare can be attributed to a lifestyle that is void of such. Just as the body needs rest on a daily basis, the soul is obliged its share as well.

Rest.

The Microcosm and Macrocosm

Greek philosophers first theorized that man is a smaller version of the universe as a whole. With this came anthropomorphism, which is the observance of human-like characteristics in non-human subjects. The subject can be living or nonliving. Together, the two concepts make up the microcosm-macrocosm philosophy. Just as a child can be seen as a smaller version of their parent, why can't we be seen as such with God? In Psalm 82:6 the author writes that we are all gods. Jesus backs this up in John 10:34 as he refers to the former scripture *"...is it not written in your law, I said, Ye are gods?"*

On earth exists many levels of change, or evolution. From the inanimate, to the most complex of beings, we are all incarnates dwelling in and working through different stages of evolvement. We share a common goal that is fueled by an indwelling yearning to be the highest version of ourselves. If one incarnate was so much greater than the next, then surely a more appropriate dwelling for that soul would have been determined. This alone is exemplary of how life on earth is a microcosm of the universe. Just as there exists multiple levels of evolvement on earth, there also exists multiple levels of evolution in the universe(s). However, it does not end there. There are multiple levels of evolvement within the human race alone, but most importantly within you yourself. You are forever changing and experiencing something new. Each new experience is a new exposure and an opportunity to embrace a new thought, one that leads to a greater version of yourself. One that yields evolvement, or better said evolution. You don't have to stay in one place in life. In fact, to do so is to work against nature. There is always a better way, and life is always presenting it to you. Think on this, has there ever been an act that you may have committed in the past, but now cannot fathom the idea of committing such again? This new thought supports an elevated change in you. That in and of itself is evolution! Just as sure as we share this earth together we all have a certain degree of evolvement that must take place. We all have internal matters to resolve, and we are all provided the circumstances by which to do so. Though most of the circumstances come in the most unwelcomed of fashions, I challenge you to see the very next one as an opportunity rather than an obstacle. Keep moving. Walk it out. Many times it will appear to be just the opposite of what it really is. Yet, whether you understand your soul's agenda or not, you are still encouraged to *"...work out your own salvation...For it is God who works in you both to will and to do of His good pleasure"* (Philippians 2:12-13). It is He who works on the inside to gift us with the will to choose a better way. We can accept or decline. Notwithstanding, there is room for us all, no matter the level of evolution.

In my Father's house are many mansions: if it were not so, I would have told you. I go to prepare a place for you.
JOHN 14:2 KJV

"A legitimate conflict between science and religion cannot exist. Science without religion is lame; religion without science is blind."
— ALBERT EINSTEIN, 1941

CHAPTER 2

Natural Laws

It is easier for heaven and earth to pass away
than for one dot of the Law to become void.
— LUKE 16:17 ESV

The Bible references *natural* laws in two ways: those written as regulations and those that govern nature and humanity. We will focus on the latter, primarily natural events and human interactions. First let's look at a reference to God's law, and then we will move into physical laws.

In Romans 2:14-15 Paul says, "*For when Gentiles who do not have the Law, these, not having the Law, are a law to themselves, in that they show the work of the law written in their hearts, their conscience bearing witness and their thoughts alternately accusing or else defending them.*" In The Message Bible it states "*When outsiders who have never heard of God's law follow it more or less by instinct, they confirm its truth by their obedience. They show that God's law is not something alien, imposed on us from without, but woven into the very fabric of our creation. There is something deep within them that echoes God's yes and no, right and wrong."* In a time where many have walked away from the faith of their parents and grandparents, this concept has never been more obvious. There are simply those that are not convinced by what they have experienced around them, and others who outright say that He is not so. However, His law still hides in their heart. There is so much more to be said of God's laws and His promises, but that is another work all by itself.

Physical laws. Even though there are many physical events that are without explanation, that is not to say that the explanation does not exist. A physical event absolutely cannot be without a physical explanation. For every physical incident there exists a dual explanation from both the physical and spiritual realm. However, for any given spiritual phenomenon, there may or may not be a physical account. For this cause, the physical aspect is second to the spiritual.

$$E = mc^2$$

Special Relativity. I have worked hard to condense this section and keep it as relatable as possible. $E=mc^2$ is by far Einstein's most famous equation. Much knowledge can be extracted from this alone, as it is very expansive. Einstein was on a quest to understand every detail of the mechanics of this world, particularly things unseen. Though his views on God and religion often conflicted, he still yearned to know the thoughts of God. "I want to know how God created this world. I want to know his thoughts." He set out to satisfy this yearning through numbers and equations. In 1905, God began to resolve his quest. Einstein discovered that in the presence of a constant (speed of light), mass is equal to energy and energy is equal to mass. For believers the latter part is more important. The equation could just as easily have been written as $E \leftrightarrow m(\text{speed of light})^2$.

Spiritual Law. In this renowned equation the speed of light is the constant, which means that it is *unchanged.* The irony is this: to effect organized change, there must always be an *unwavering* constant. Yes, the Word. Hebrews 11:1 addresses faith as the substance of things hoped for (mass), and the evidence of things not seen (energy). Now that the importance of a constant is understood, let us focus on $E \leftrightarrow m$. Essentially, the equation is saying that where there is a constant energy and mass are equal. Where there is a certain energy there also is its equivalent mass, vice versa. Briefly, here's how we can apply this in our practical lives:

FOR EVERYTHING THAT OCCUPIES SPACE IN YOUR
LIFE IT CAN BE DISMANTLED
BY A SIMILAR ENERGY,
AND
FOR EVERY ENERGY (THOUGHT, MOOD) THAT YOU
CONTAIN IT WILL REPRODUCE ITSELF PHYSICALLY.

Footnote: [E/energy; M/mass (anything that takes up space); C/constant, in this case the speed of light]. The spiritual application for this equation may be used intentionally or unintentionally; favorably or unfavorably.

It is just that simple. Where there is energy the corresponding mass will be expressed physically. Used intentionally and wisely, the theory of E=mc² is a great gift to mankind and all great ones have used it in prayer. So can you. "...the works that I do shall he do also" (John 14:12 KJV). Surely, this section begs for expansion, but I am compelled to leave it here.

Conservation of Energy

Everything is energy. Whether it be directly or indirectly, all energy comes from the sun. This includes the very energy that you are using to read these words. All energy on earth has been present since the beginning of creation and is conserved within our "isolated system." This means that energy cannot be added or taken away. Therefore, all of the energy necessary has been provided for since the beginning of time and remains constant. This can not be changed without some combustible event. However, it can be disrupted. For more on this read on greenhouse gases. Another, more practical, disruption is how we lay our loved ones to rest. Can you imagine the energy that would be returned to the system if we did not use impenetrable enclosures?

According to the First Law of Thermodynamics, "Energy can neither be created nor destroyed, but can be transformed from one form to another." Despite the fact that we are in an *isolated system*, and no energy can be added, there is a great deal of interplay between present energies. Though there is no loss or gain, energy can be transformed. It can change its complete composure. The next time you are angry, work less to attempt to rid the energy, but instead move to transform it into something more constructive. Energy can also be transferred. This concept may be applied in many aspects of life, favorable or not. Using the same example of anger, this energy can easily be transferred to another person. Take a young child who grows up in a household of contention and abuse. That energy can be transferred to that child, and if it shows up readily it may manifest as a neurological disorder. This is a condition known as somatization disorder. Soma means body. In this condition, the stressful condition induces symptoms with no obvious physical abnormality. There have been many documented cases of patients experiencing neurological disorders, such as seizures and blindness, following extensive emotional stress. In the great majority of cases, once the stress is removed the symptoms disappear. When it comes to transference of energy, the same can be said of the energy that we call love. It can be transferred in such a way that the same magnitude of energy it takes to create it, such will be required to disassemble it.

The two primary forms of energy are potential and kinetic, inactive and active energy, respectively. In potential energy, the energy is stored up and its effects cannot be readily appreciated. It needs some external force to act on it such that it may be converted to the active form, kinetic energy. Kinetic energy is energy in motion. This form of energy packs heat! The heat from this energy can be transferred to any other entity in its vicinity, or anything by which it interacts. These two forms may show up in nearly any manner. Let us focus on human behavior and interactions. Ecclesiastes 1:9 KJV says, *"The thing that hath been, it is that which shall be; and that which is done is that which shall be done: and there is no new thing under the sun."* Here Solomon explains that whatever thing that happened in the past (hath been) will happen again in the future (shall be); and the same deeds of times past shall be committed again. Every current event that you are witnessing or have ever read about has taken place before, even as far back as prehistoric times. We have always operated under the same energy since the beginning of time. There has always been the energy of love, creativity, unity, joy, loyalty, betrayal, grief, contention, murder, pride, hate, bitterness, jealousy, etc. that have all played out in various forms in accordance with the current affairs of that time. So it is indeed the same game, but with different tools and different players. This is why you've heard it said so many times that "history repeats itself." Nothing is new. For every experience that exists there is a pattern by which it takes place. Commonly these patterns are duplicated in many aspects of life. The Bible displays every energy form and emotion that may be experienced by mankind. It is a compilation of relatable events and inspirational narratives. The story of Jesus exhibits the most powerful of them all: Love. However, there are countless stories that represent other emotions such as betrayal. Recall the stories of both Joseph and Jesus. Fear is represented in the story of Peter walking on water. Courage is exemplified when David was tasked with taking down

Goliath. Note, all of those same energies exist today. Again, energy can be neither created or destroyed, but instead it takes on different forms in different vectors being transformed or transferred from one thing to the next. The person who gives no thought to their actions, does no research prior to their conclusion becomes an easy vector for energy transference. Just observe the current times. Once again, there is no thing that is new under the sun. However, know this: we are not without escape.

◦◦◦

Zeroth Law of Thermodynamics

The Zeroth Law of Thermodynamics states that if two thermo-dynamic systems are each in thermal equilibrium with a third, then they are in thermal equilibrium with each other. In other words, there are three energetic and kinetic systems working in sync with each other. In John 10:30 KJV Jesus says, *"I and my Father are One."* This represents the equilibrium of the first two systems. In John 15:26 NKJV, Jesus says, *"But when the Helper comes, whom I shall send to you from the Father, the Spirit of truth who proceeds from the Father, He will testify of me."* In this passage Jesus acknowledges equilibrium with yet a third entity. This is the Oneness of the holy trinity. All things spoken of the Holy Spirit are in equilibrium with God. We can also think of it in terms of corporate prayer with kindred spirits, as there is considerable power in unity of like-minded individuals.

*For where two or three are gathered together in
my name, there am I in the midst of them.*
— MATTHEW 18:20 KJV

It is worth noting that such energy, through concentrated fervent prayer, has the power to be transformational. Yet, it may also be *transferred*. This has the potential to be extraordinarily useful, or it could be perilous. Transferred energy, when done so by truly faith-filled individuals, can and does bring about healing and deliverance.

However, here is another side to consider. Ever had a conversation with someone who was so convincing they caused you to believe in a thing against your better judgement? In psychology there is a diagnosis known as "shared psychotic disorder." The French call it "folie à deux," or the folly of two. Shared psychotic disorder is when there is the primary patient with established psychosis who has convinced someone else with whom he/she has an emotional connection. The second person has an unremarkable mental health history and, up until this point, has lived a fairly normal life. His/her symptoms are more alarming in the presence of, or following recent contact with, the primary patient. Symptoms tend to subside with loss of contact with the primary patient. This is a prime example of energy transference. Also, see Chapter 11 on *mirror neurons*.

Path of Least Resistance

This is nature's near effortless means of "going with the flow." The path of least resistance is indeed a natural way of conserving energy. Least resistance means that which opposes the least, thereby requiring the slightest amount of energy expenditure. Particularly from a metaphysical standpoint, there has been much written about this. For said reason we are forced to use a Janus-faced approach with it. There is no set means of reflecting on this concept. Let us start with what Jesus says of it in Matthew 7:13-14 KJV:

> *Enter ye in at the strait gate: for wide is the gate, and broad is the way, that leadeth to destruction, and many there be which go in thereat: Because strait is the gate, and narrow is the way, which leadeth unto life, and few there be that find it.*

What does He mean by the wide gate leading to destruction? The wide gate of course, would be the way that is subject to the least amount of opposition and requires the least amount of effort. Now let us consider destruction. This is the dismantling of that which has been organized. Yet, even with this, the wide gate retains its popularity. Fewer choose the straight or narrow gate, as it is often times out of view or not readily available. More obviously, it may require more effort, more prayer. Nonetheless, this is the path that availeth much. This is the path to life, and life more abundantly.

Ever noticed when you have been praying for something and you start noticing a knockoff version of your prayer request first? Initially you question it, then decide to move forward with the receipt of it. This is least resistance at work. Whatever thoughts you have organized through your prayer about it will begin to be dismantled. May it be boldly noted, this does not necessarily mean that your life will now go to ruins. It simply means that what you initially began to create for yourself will no longer be. Many will then commence the process of adjusting down to accommodate this new version of their request. However, you do not have to settle for it. Keep your faith. Stay the course. Your genuine answer is on its way.

Here is yet another example. Imagine this, we have a man with a hole in his pocket. His wife has been urging him to allow her to repair it, but he never gets around to it. By the way, truth will always nudge us. Nonetheless, he often dismisses her concern and forgets about the hole. Out of daily habit he continues to place his money in his pocket. One particular day while on a store run for his wife, his path crosses that of a college student. The student is barely making ends meet and has been in prayer concerning his finances. This does not go unnoticed. Think it not strange that he finds two twenty dollar bills rolled up on the ground in the parking lot with no one around with whom to return them. Here we have the epitome of harmony between blessings and misfortunes. Please note, when given the opportunity it will serve you well to take the necessary steps to identify the owner of loss money or valuables whenever possible. Remember in Matthew 7:12 KJV Jesus says, *"Therefore all things whatsoever ye would that men should do to you: do ye even so to them: for this is the law and the prophets.*" However, when it is of a divine plan you would be at a loss to find a legitimate soul to which it belongs.

Cause and Effect

Cause and effect is a natural law and understanding it is very important. In fact, it is a very dangerous thing to ignore the natural sequence of events simply because you have no experience in it or that you do not believe that it can happen to you. This is not to say do not have faith. Indeed, keep the faith, as adequate faith will divert the events that are to befall you. However, *when understanding* your circumstances be rational. Be calculated. What has obviously come upon you should not be dismissed or ignored. There is a natural order to *all* phenomenon, and nature may proceed with or without your belief in her. Never become reckless about something because you feel that it will not happen to you. Do not substitute your rational mind to comfort yourself in foolish ways in the name of faith. That is not faith. True faith is always preceded by the acknowledgement, or possibility of an undesirable condition. Yet you *know* that He stands ready to intervene on your behalf. For example, faith does not rise from ignoring a grim medical diagnosis, but is instead forged through acknowledgement of, as the saying goes, "what could've, should've or would've been" had it not been for Him thwarting natural laws in interest of you. For more on faith refer to Chapter 12.

❧

Resolution

Ever noticed when an airplane is making its descent and the objects below become more visible? At some point prior the objects were barely distinguishable and the boundaries that define them were ambiguous. When viewing objects through a light microscope the goal is to see each tiny object as distinctly and clearly as possible. This is when the term resolution comes in. Resolution means that when viewing two small objects that are side by side the space between them may be appreciated just enough to see them as distinct objects instead of one big blur. However, sometimes this poses a challenge. To overcome this, it becomes necessary to magnify the area of concern, the focal area, by going up to a higher power. This increases the microscope's ability to resolve that which is occupying space, the matter. The higher the power, the greater the ability to resolve. If you want the best resolution, tap into the highest power.

And if I go and prepare a place for you, I will come again and receive you to Myself; that where I am, there you may be also.

— John 14:3 NKJV

CHAPTER 3

Jesus Christ

And the Word became flesh,
and dwelt among us…
— JOHN 1:14 NKJV

God is the creator of all things. However, one of the most difficult things to accept is that God created evil. In fact, it is regularly omitted simply because it is poorly understood. As it happens, the greatest hindrance and limitation to our spiritual growth is that we worship and serve God within the confines of our own beliefs. There are sects that will embrace God's grace and mercy, and there are others who simply adore the messages of His wrath. Know this: He is all of it and everything in between. Do not be so caught up in the wrath and judgment that you fail to see His limitless loving heart, His grace and mercy *to all*. Do not be so captivated by His loving heart that you fail to see the natural order of things. God created it all. God is all. Again, Isaiah 45:7 KJV says,

I form the light, and create darkness: I make peace, and create evil. I the Lord do all these things.

Grasping this allows for a better understanding of Jesus Christ. The title Christ is Greek for "anointed one." It is Hebrew for "messiah." Imagine God the Father as the stern, matter-of-fact parent who does everything perfectly and by the book without fail. But did you know that this authoritative parent has another side? This side of God once walked the earth. Jesus Christ was an incarnate of God.

I and my Father are one.
— JOHN 10:30 KJV

He is the Word of God. He *is* the loving version of God. He is the sacrificial lamb of God and through His compassion, He takes away the sin of the world (John 1:29). There is no thing that can not be healed through the greatest compassion known to man, Jesus Christ. Enlightened well beyond His era, He was humanity's most prized gift. He came to render salvation to us by conforming to a shape that was complementary to humankind. Once we accept and carry out the teachings of Christ, our life becomes a light in the world.

Jesus saith unto him, I am the way,
the truth, and the life: no man cometh
unto the Father, but by me.
— JOHN 14:6 KJV

Unfortunately, this has been widely misunderstood and has been misused as a basis of religious intolerance for centuries. This scripture should not be used to justify such. In fact, Jesus advocates that we tolerate other religions. Yes. Recall when John complains of witnessing another who was not of their fold casting out demons.

> ...*Master, we saw one casting out devils in thy name; and we forbad him, because he followeth not with us. And Jesus said unto him, Forbid him not: for he that is not against us is for us.*
> — LUKE 9:49-50 KJV

It is hypercritical that we understand Jesus's response. Here He corrects his disciples against intolerance. John was obviously bothered and could not conceive how someone could exemplify such power apart from Jesus' fold. The stranger must have been a fraud. Jesus realigns this method of thinking when He says, "he that is not against us is for us." If he is not clearly against love, compassion, enlightenment, etc., and all that Jesus symbolizes, then he is with us. His religion may have a separate method of worship. Her Bible may be filled with inspirational events and relatable stories that you have never heard. Yet, if love and oneness is at the center of their practice, then against such there is no law. The rest are just details and Bible fillers. And that's okay. Take note: sometimes the Word has to be delivered in a different fashion. Such is why we have various denominations. Sometimes the Word is better served using different stories and characters. Such is why there are assorted religions. Sometimes the Word must be rational and its messengers must be very trustworthy. Such is why we have atheists.

I am the way: There are numerous variants of Jesus' teachings shared by many organized religions. Love, compassion, and the path to enlightenment may be addressed by different names, but their principles remain unchanged. In fact, many of these teachings preceded His incarnation on earth. The Old Testament is just one example of a collection of Christ-like teachings that preceded Him. Nonetheless, there was obviously cause for reinforcement. He came not only to remind us, but to exemplify the way. During His incarnation He demonstrated the way through Word and through deed. No man shall ever reach that heavenly state except by the likes of His teachings. Except by Him.

I am the truth: The Word of God is law. It is the truth. Jesus represents the Word of God in flesh form, and not only did He convey messages of eternal truths, but so were His deeds. Everything that He said came to pass, and everything that He did was done under the anointing of God. "*...For on Him God the Father has set His seal*" (John 6:27 ESV). He is the truth! And Jesus has shared and is still sharing that same truth with us today. John 14:12 says, "*...He that believeth on me, the works that I do shall he do also; and greater works than these shall he do...*"

I am the life: Here Jesus speaks of life on a different plane. He is referring to an abundant flow of energy that never ceases, everlasting life. This indicates that through Him and implementation of His teachings you will have access to such. Recall, not all of Jesus's teachings are limited to the Bible. They are pervasive across many religions and their doctrines. Whether He is acknowledged by name or not, any teaching that is based on compassion and love reverberates the spirit of Jesus Christ. A fervent desire to implement His teachings comes with opportunities to do such, i.e. trials and tribulations. During these times it is so important to eat of His bread. In John 6:35 Jesus says, *"I am the bread of life."* So continue to fight the good fight. This is the key to life and life more abundantly.

CHAPTER 4

The Molecular Parallel

Matter is anything that has mass and occupies space, and an atom is the smallest unit of matter. Chemicals are always reacting around us. Bonds are constantly being formed and others being broken. However, the breaking of bonds actually releases energy. Think about a relation in the beginning and the break up. This is chemistry, and as the arrangement of atoms become more advanced it yields life. A fully developed adult is made up of an average of 100 trillion cells. Each cell is specialized to function within a given facet. Cells are grouped together based on their likeness and their functionality. Those nearest to each other are related , as they perform similar functions, if not the same. These cells are more likely to be a part of the same tissue, organ, or systems. The farther away they are the less likely they are related. Often, the closer cells may have different but complementary functions. Sounds a lot like family? In order for the cells to perform any action outside of their normal routine they must first have permission from the control center, or the nervous system. This permission is granted when the cell is approached by a chemical with a recognizable composition. There is a specific chemical for distinct cells in particular conditions that will render a precise response. This chemical must con*form* to a certain con*figur*ation so that it will be received and acknowledged by the target cell. This sophisticated process takes place with a high degree of precision and fidelity. This is absolutely the only way that the chemical, and therefore message, will be received by the cell. Once the message is received the cell will respond accordingly, as it benefits the cell to do so. It is this exact process that has allowed you to thrive since birth. Such is the case with the Word of God. John 1:14 KJV states *"...the Word was made flesh, and dwelt among us, (and we beheld His glory, the glory as of the only begotten of the Father,) full of grace and truth."* The Word became embodied by Jesus Christ, a being of recognizable form, who came to deliver powerful messages. There are clear benefits to understanding the messages and teachings of Christ. John 3:16 KJV states *"For God so loved the world that He gave His only begotten Son, that whosoever believeth in Him should not perish, but have everlasting life."*

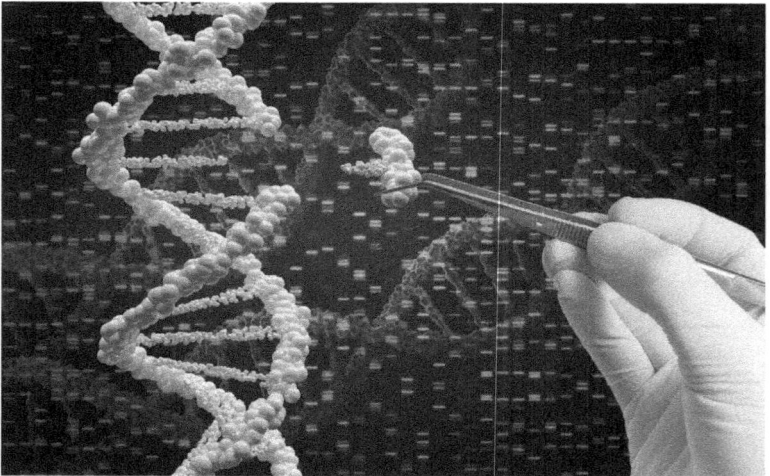

"Jesus will come in and reset your DNA."
— Minister, Open Door Christian Faith
Worship Center -Montgomery, AL

CHAPTER 5

Genetics

❧❧

*For you created my inmost being; you knit me
together in my mother's womb. I praise you
because I am fearfully and wonderfully made;
your works are wonderful, I know that full well.*
— PSALMS 139:13-14 NIV

❧❧

Computer coding involves aligning a series of keystrokes to effect a certain outcome. Each character must be specifically placed to render a particular task. Any error could yield a malfunction. The same happens with our DNA. Though modifiable, we are coded to respond a certain way to our environment. Our genes are arranged in a distinct way to assure this. This meticulous arrangement we call our genotype. Our DNA can then delegate what it would like to have happen by making discrete proteins to carry out its duties. Production of these precise proteins is what decodes the language of DNA. This is how genes express themselves. When you look at a person you are viewing the external pressing (expression) of their genes. This is called phenotype. As a personal coach I have been able to provide sound counsel simply by observing, for example, the shape of someone's hands, nose, or lips. Every phenotypic feature is with reason, some greater than others. Your physical attributes are external expressions of your genetic code. Your genetic code is the physical declaration of your spiritual journey.

In biology there is the concept of natural selection. It is as if Mother Nature selects the traits that best suits you for the environment that you are in. The changes are typically observed over generations. However, in a recent twin study conducted by NASA, astronaut and identical twin Scott Kelly did a one year tour into space. His genes were analyzed before, during, and after his tour. It was observed that the stress from such a drastic change in his environment caused his genetic expression to be altered. Furthermore 7% of his genes did not return to their original baseline after two years of having returned to earth. Though he and his twin brother Mark are still considered identical twins, they now have a slight discrepancy in their genetic makeup. Nonetheless, the notable point is that gene expression may be altered. Though it causes a much more rapid alteration in gene expression when survival is at stake, stress is not the only influencer of gene expression. It may be modified depending on the circumstances or immediate environment. Does this mean that an adopted child can express genes similar to that of her adopted parents? To some degree, yes! Does this mean that if a male child is much closer to his mother, that it could cause him to upregulate more of her genes, including those on his X chromosome? Entirely so! For more on this see Chapter 14. Take a native girl from Puerto Rico who moves to Alaska for a new job. The genes that are responsible for the production of melanin will now be down-regulated, as there will be a decrease in the need for them. Our body is constantly taking inventory and responding accordingly. The response, more often than not, is one that will enhance survival, even if for a short time. It happens subconsciously more often than we realize. I once heard a preacher say that Jesus will come in and reset your DNA. Could this be true? Absolutely! What's more, *"...He that believeth on me, the works that I do shall he do also"* (John 14:12). You can too. How exceptional is it to know that you have conscious control over your gene expression as well! In this book I will limit this discussion to a select few practical examples. Nonetheless, you indeed can alter your gene expression depending on your circumstances. Some of these genes are classified as *maintenance* genes, and their degree of expression is constantly changing in accordance with our needs. Something as simple as changing your diet can alter your gene expression. The concept of natural selection explains just how the body, more accurately genes, responds to the environment. You can be even more proactive in this, as in many cases altering your environment can be influential enough to cause your genetic expression to adjust. How empowering is that!

There can never be another you. You could have been at least 7 trillion other people. Meaning that from the moment your mother's egg and father's sperm cell united there were 7 trillion possibilities for your full genetic complement. There were ancestral genes all competing to be externally pressed *through you.* This is because you are a carrier of the genetic code that has persisted since the beginning of time. Ideally, this code should be advanced with each successive generation. That is why, embedded within our genome exists a modified code of all other life forms. However, this is when natural selection takes place. This is a more universal approach to understanding gene expression. Typically, those genes that are relevant to an individual's environment and are able to enhance survival in the same are the ones that are chosen. With all factors considered, including genes and survival, what you see in the mirror is what nature deemed as best suited for you.

And then there is your gift. We are reminded in James 1:17 NIV that *"Every good and perfect gift is from above, coming down from the Father of the heavenly lights, who does not change like shifting shadows."* In each of us exists an area of concentration- an area where God seemed to have concentrated more of Himself. It is an area where He graced us with the ability to enter into His presence with much greater ease. The moment that we tap into that area, our focus narrows. We become more aware of our oneness with Him. It is your key. It is your anointing, and is coded for and concentrated in your genetic makeup. Though when you hear the term "anointed" it is typically limited to religious worthy-talents or gifts. I invite you to expand that point of view. For example, Tua Tagovailoa has a remarkable ability to filter out nonsense mental noise while swiftly prioritizing incoming data. This allows him to execute a play with extraordinary precision. Though he has made no secret of his spiritual walk, his gift is highlighted on the field. He is anointed and surely such focused talent can be used to edify the kingdom.

Just as humans have 99.9% of the same genetic material, all cells have the exact same DNA, but not all will express the same genes. They all have general maintenance genes called housekeeping genes. Their purpose is more of a supportive one, yet it is still very important. However, certain cells will express both housekeeping genes and tissue-specific genes. Just as our cells are capable of upregulating other genes, we have what it takes to express genes beyond our imagining. In a glorified sense, we all have near the same potential. However, some genes are more active in some than others. This can change. It would serve us all well to know that.

Family. How beautiful is it when individuals with similar genes express themselves as one unit! This is family. It might be easy to recognize certain trends in a given family, such as successes and misfortunes. However, it's not too surprising to hear of individuals who are of close relation going through similar things around the same time. In fact, the closer you are and the more you have in common, the more likely the occurrence. Sometimes related individuals have to fight the same demons, or they have to face some of the same challenges. This is commonly referred to as "generational curses." Commonly a misfortune will befall one person before it happens in the other, i.e. parent, older sibling, aunt, uncle, cousin, etc. Your task as family is to seek guidance through prayer and stand firmly on the loving Word thereafter. This is how you clear the path for those who are to come behind you, lest you lead them into the same ways of error. Let that be of encouragement for you. Moreover, if you are that younger relative, and you witnessed a family member go through major challenges but through sound prayer and faithfulness to the Word they overcame that challenge, then when the same presents itself to you, take the path that has already been cleared for you! In this way, family will strengthen family.

Remember *all* living beings across all three domains share some degree of genetic makeup and are of the same source. Therefore, we have common ancestry with even your house plant. This alone is cause enough to value all life.

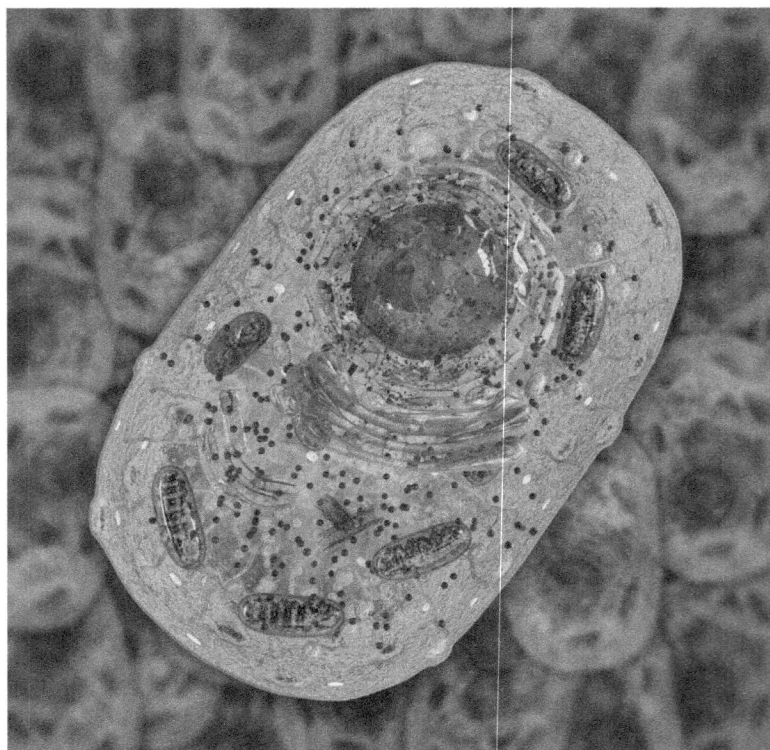

All things were made by Him; and without Him was not any thing made that was made.
— JOHN 1:3 KJV

CHAPTER 6

The Cellular Level of Creation

In science, we describe a living organism as anything that has the ability to move, take in nourishment, respond to its environment, release waste, exchange vital gases, or reproduce. Organisms must display some degree of these characteristics to be characterized as living. Prior to the 1860s it was an acceptable thought that life impulsively generated from thin air, a theory known as Spontaneous Generation. This notion was later disproven and replaced by the modern day Cell Theory. The Cell Theory states that the smallest unit of life is at the level of the cell, and that all cells had to have been derived from a parent cell. That is to say, life begets life. We are of Him. We are made in His likeness as a child is to her parent. In Genesis we see that on the third day simpler life begins to form. Scientists theorize that the first cell may have existed over 3.5 billion years, and that all other cells have derived from said cell. The genomics of life has evolved ever since.

Inside of the cell. The cytoplasm is the medium by which all of the cell's organelles are embedded. It nourishes the cell and has all of the nutrients needed for the basic functions by the cell's components. If ever the organelles are in need of a certain nutrition all they have to do is open themselves up to receive it. Of course, this is done by instinct and requires absolutely no thought. This is the system in place by the cells. You are composed of 100 trillion of these faithful units. There is no doubt that you carry the same capacity. Align yourself such that you may receive it.

We are but a cell in the universe; a grain of sand in the ocean. However, inside these seemingly infinite units are chemicals and structures that support their vitality. Among the important internal structures of the cell is yet an even more important element, the nucleus. The cell can do nothing without the nucleus. Within it is all of the genetic material to cause the cell to function a certain way, to make the necessary proteins that the entire body will benefit from. For this reason, the nucleus is also referred to as the "brain of the cell."

One operative, or inoperative cell can start a series of reactions that can make or break the body as a whole. We are well aware that cancer starts as one rogue cell. This cell has a dysfunctional nucleus with mutated genetics. It proliferates quickly by producing clones of itself. Before long it, along with its clones gain visibly, and are now influential enough to sway the body's resources toward itself. Departing from the sequela of cancer a bit, let us now say that this rogue cell represents an individual. This one individual has the ability to hurt others who are weak enough to succumb to his impartation. They will follow suit.

Your outermost skin cells are continuously exposed to toxins in the environment. That same layer of cells update and replace themselves every 4-6 weeks. When you look at those cells six weeks from now you will literally be looking at a replenished version of yourself. How relieving is that! Their capabilities are a microcosm of your own. You can literally shed any superficial layer of your being and reinvent yourself anew and there is nothing anyone can do about it. Never be afraid to recreate yourself for the better.

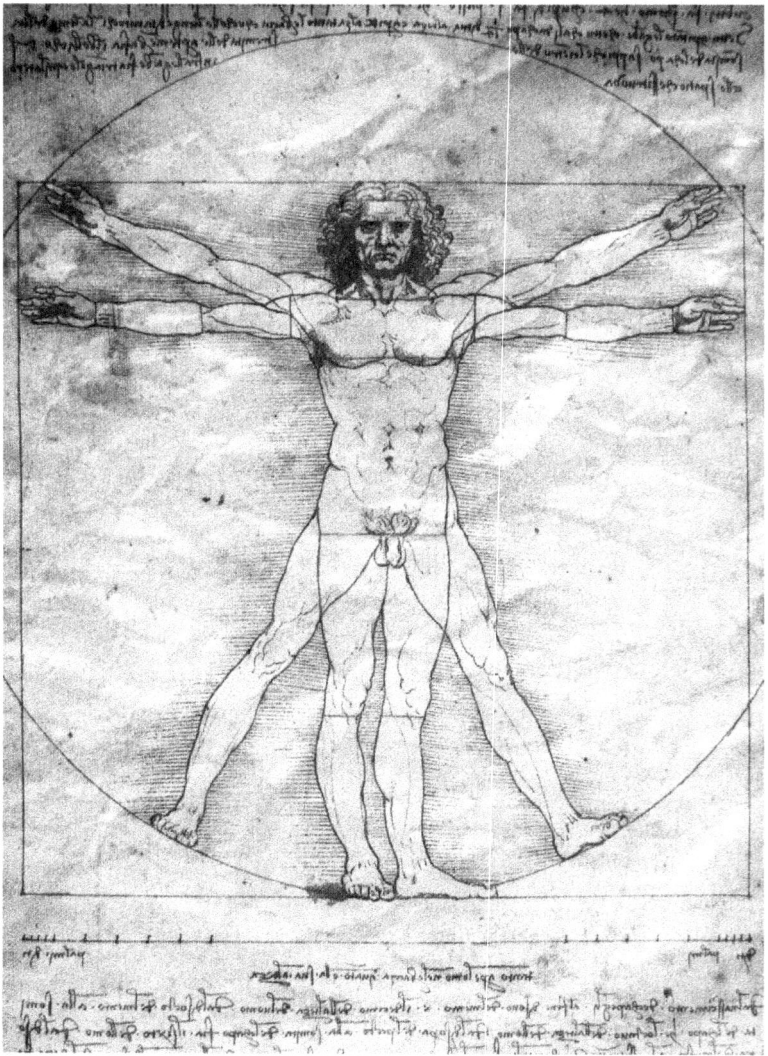

CHAPTER 7

The Body

Know ye not that ye are the temple of God,
and that the Spirit of God dwelleth in you?
— 1 CORINTHIANS 3:16 KJV

1 Corinthians 12 is all about the body of Christ and the church! We are all incarnates on earth. By that alone we have a certain degree of challenges, and no one soul can be esteemed above another. The mere fact that he/she is here on earth speaks volumes of their level of evolvement as well as their level of need. Therefore, it is imperative that we allow Him to live through us. The body is the incarnate by which the soul dwells. The soul experiences physicality through the body. Our soul, a fragment of the Great Soul, is our connection to God. Therefore God experiences life through you. One of the many differences between us and Jesus is that He was distinctly aware of His connection. *"I and my Father are One"* (John 10:30 KJV). Now imagine yourself with that same sense of lucidity regarding your relationship with the Father. It is *not* too good to be true. It is simply true. In the midst of all that we carry throughout life let Him be God. Let Him come through your many roles and life labels. Some of us are heavily attached to our past life experiences, or even those of our forefathers. Intentionally allow God to experience what it is like to carry these labels and watch how He manages. Allow Him to flow through you and work through it. Understanding our oneness with God better allows us to be conduits of His many blessings.

The philosopher Aristotle once said, "The whole is greater than the sum of its parts." Therefore the body truly is greater than its individual parts. Likewise, so is the body of Christ. We are Great and much stronger together.

> *(Christ) From whom the whole body fitly joined*
> *together and compacted by that which every joint*
> *supplieth, according to the effectual working in*
> *the measure of **every part, maketh increase***
> ***of the body** unto the edifying of itself in love.*
> — EPHESIANS 4:16 KJV

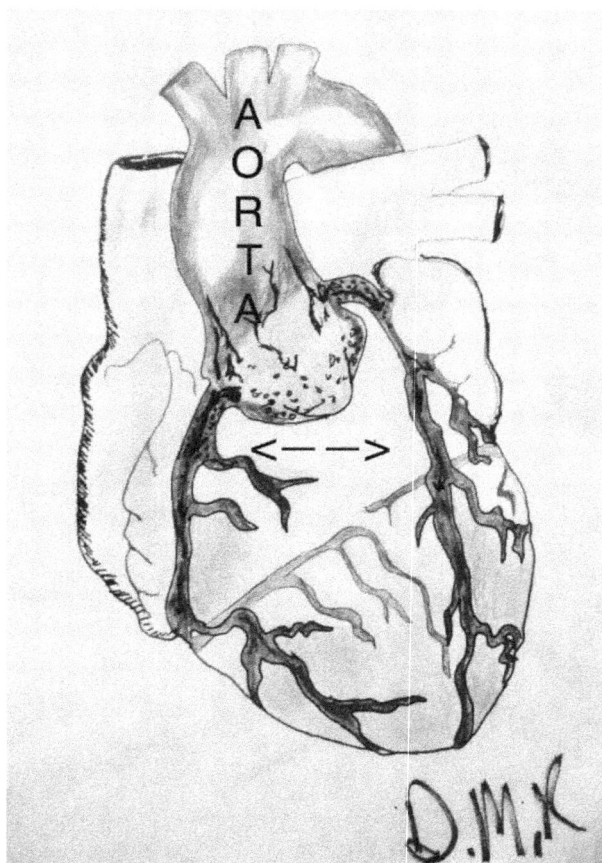

Let not your heart be troubled...
— John 14:1 KJV

CHAPTER 8

The Cardiovascular System

Keep thy heart with all diligence; for
out of it are the issues of life.
— Proverbs 4:23 KJV

It goes without saying that the heart is a very important muscle in the body. It takes care of everyone else, but who's taking care of the heart? It is noble to perform selfless acts, to be caring, and to be loving. However, for some it must be stated, do not neglect yourself, or you will soon become of little to no use to anyone else, or the kingdom for that matter. Useless. Sounds harsh? Well, think of it another way. The next time that you are preparing for take-off and the flight attendant demonstrates to you the order in which you should don your oxygen mask, take note of how she emphasizes that you must put your mask on first before helping anyone else. Some airlines will even play videos to further illustrate the necessity of the parent putting his mask on first before assisting his child with their mask. Before the heart sends nourishing blood to any other part of the body, it immediately sends it to itself first. Yes, the heart takes care of itself first. This is done by way of a set of encircling arteries called the coronary arteries. When these arteries become compromised the heart is no longer efficient in supplying itself with highly oxygenated blood. The body's ability to satisfy its basic needs becomes greatly compromised. The body could die. Therefore, the heart knows that if it takes care of itself first then it will have the means to care for others. This is not to be taken out of context. Always be certain that your own basic needs for survival are met first.

What goes around comes around. What you put out is what you get back. A healthy heart will always circulate a certain minimum amount of blood. This is vital. Life would not continue in the absence of this process. As well oxygenated blood circulates its ultimate purpose is to supply the tissues with sufficient oxygen. This helps to revitalize the cells so that they can thrive and function properly. This flux of blood may be likened to spreading love.

In the absence of blood *there is no life*. Depending on the severity, disruption of the circulatory system may cause malfunction of the entire body. However, when the disruption is global the brain is among the first to show overt signs. Without love so is the same. When there is a lack of love it is typically most evident through one's perspective. That is not to say that everyone with a mental illness was not loved as a child. No. However, if a child is assured of love, the risk is minimal. Remember the nervous system, the control center of the body, is most responsive to love in the first few years of life. There has been much research on this topic.

Above all, love each other deeply, because love covers over a multitude of sins.
— 1 PETER 4:8 NIV

The circulatory system not only provides nutrients, but healing factors as well. Our white blood cells can shape shift and sacrifice themselves leaving an area of protection, the blood, to enter into a hostile inflamed and/or infected area. This is where they are needed. Their sole purpose is to heal. Sound familiar? For this reason, all living cells must be less than 1 mm from a capillary. This allows for easy access to nutrients and of course, healing factors. Always stay close to the Word for the same. Know this: when one cell is in need the circulatory system will modify the body's hemodynamics. It will alter the course of blood flow such that the one cell in need is served. Yes, one cell. One single cell can release chemicals called cytokines that will cause a relative amount of blood to be rerouted toward itself.

How think ye? if a man have an hundred sheep, and one of them be gone astray, doth he not leave the ninety and nine, and goeth into the mountains, and seeketh that which is gone astray?
— MATTHEW 18:12 KJV

Because of the average size of our individual cells, this healing feature is inferred based on a grander scale observation. In other words, this feature is more evident when a larger number of cells are affected. For example, if you accidentally scratch yourself with a safety pin in a matter of seconds you will be able to observe changes. Mild swelling and redness are both evidence of increased blood flow to the area. This reaction is known as inflammation. The ultimate purpose of short term inflammation is healing, and the body will refocus its hemodynamics, namely blood flow, in effort to save the one (or more).

Stress

When you are under stress the sympathetic nervous system is activated and the body thinks it is about to die. Indeed, it goes into survival mode. This starts in your mind and the information is immediately passed on to your cardiovascular system. The cardiovascular system faithfully responds, as it is designed to do. The focus is now on running for your life. The blood pressure increases to favor the skeletal muscles. They become tense in preparation for flight. The blood vessels constrict as to effect rapid flow to the muscles and the heart rate increases for the same reason. This literally happens. This reaction can be short-lived or acute, as in response to someone stepping on your brand new pair of shoes. Or this response can be long-term or chronic. By the way, always make the attempt to *forgo* the effect of an unfavorable act of another towards you.

Forgive. Surely you've heard many times now, *forgiveness* is for you. If you are still not convinced, then reread the beginning of this section. Nonetheless, bodily disruptions that are insidious and have more time invested are much more difficult to undo. From a physical standpoint, these have a greater likelihood of being irreversible. For example, let's say that your job has had you nearly pulling your hair out. Now when this rough day at work is over and you lie in bed to rest for the night all you can sense is your heart pumping hard and striving to force blood through constricted vessels. You can't turn off the rush. The tension in your body is too high. The moment you appear to be falling asleep your body jerks you out of it. Remember you're in survival mode. You have been running on a clock all day. When you're at work numbers matter. The left column and the right column must match. The body thinks it's about to die! You can't sleep, at least not deep sleep. If this continues past two weeks, the body may well perform a reset on its hemodynamics and this hypertensive response may become the new norm. During stressful times, please take a breather and tell yourself that it is not the end of the world, because it's not. Breathe.

> *A merry heart doeth good like a medicine...*
> — PROVERBS 17:22 KJV

Fear is the beginning of mental anguish and stress. Fear breeds unwarranted doubt. Doubt is one word for double-mindedness which has a far more pervasive effect. Double-mindedness causes you to create an alternative outcome that is in stark contrast to God's Word and His promises to you. In other words, doubt stands in conflict with the truth. So fret not, but *"Delight thyself also in the Lord; and He shall give thee the desires of thine heart"* (Psalms 37:4). Dare not place yourself on a lower thought level than this. Dare not create any other outcome. Give no other thought the time of day. Clear your throat and chase it out. Out with doubt! (See section on doubt.)

Everyone who competes in the games
goes into strict training. They do it to get
a crown that will not last, but we do it
to get a crown that will last forever.
— 1 CORINTHIANS 9:25

CHAPTER 9

The Musculoskeletal System

෴

*It shall be health to thy navel
and marrow to thy bones.*
— PROVERBS 3:8 KJV

෴

Muscular System

The muscles attached to the skeletal system are known as skeletal muscles. These are a very demanding group of muscles in that whenever they are active they insist upon more blood flow, and if they do not get it, they throw a tantrum in the form of a cramp. That is why it is advised to prime these muscles by stretching before activity. Nonetheless, the more active these muscles become, the more blood flows their way. Vital nutrients, namely oxygen, are extracted from the blood to supply them with what they need all because they insisted upon it. In fairly healthy states this happens with high fidelity and very little resistance. Let us say that you are now attempting to turn over a new leaf in your life. You are embarking on a completely new venture of sorts. The more that you make the statement of the new you, the new venture, the further you are able to extract wisdom and resources by which to accomplish this. This response will always be faithful to you, lest you begin to over-process what is taking place.

But my God shall supply all your need according to his riches in glory by Christ Jesus.
— PHILIPPIANS 4:19 KJV

Just as sure as there exists an ego, that which assures its survival, there is a psyche to defend it. Violent and defensive thoughts exist throughout the human race, in and between all ethnicities, without exception. However, the thoughts or actions may be carried out differently. The execution of violent thoughts in its most untainted form manifests itself in accordance with genetic makeup, turn physical capabilities, or lack thereof. That which lacks the physical attributes, i.e. muscularity, compensates by utilization of tools. This person typically places little to no stock in their physical capabilities. That one which tends to be more physically endowed may be more hands on. He who may not be equipped in either department may choose a more mindful or mental approach. All of the above comparisons are statements based on observations of less advanced societies. The more advanced a society, the more blurred the lines become. Nonetheless, no matter the modality of the responses they are all acts of violence.

❧

Skeletal System

I once attended a garden workshop and the presenter said that sometimes you have to "pat your plants." I thought is was a very peculiar statement, but she went on to explain how it helps them to grow more sturdy stems. I immediately thought of the skeletal system and how exercising the muscles helps to strengthen the bones. As the muscles contract during exercise they are actually pulling and tugging on the surface of the bone. This encourages designated bone cells to reinforce the bone. This is accomplished by laying down more calcium, which results in stronger bones. The same happens to us in life. Life pulls and tugs on us, and without realizing it our inner core becomes fortified in the process. If you give it a bit of thought you will see how there are things in times past that formerly caused you great stress, and now they don't. You have already been strengthened in many ways. Allow the process to continue.

CHAPTER 10

The Digestive System

‧◦‧

Do not work for food that spoils, but for food
that endures to eternal life, which the Son
of Man will give you. For on him God the
Father has placed His seal of approval.
— JOHN 6:27 NIV

‧◦‧

H ave you ever been around food but were in no position to eat at that moment? Yet, you were hungry. At the very thought of food, let alone the sight or smell, the body begins to prepare to receive it. A series of physiological reactions will take place, many of which may be easily observed. Gastric juices are released. Bowel activity increases making the abdomen "growl." The parotid glands begin to release saliva. All of this happens in preparation for the receipt of a snack, or a meal. We are so powerful that with the very thought of food the body starts preparing for the receipt of it. Yet, this requires no conscious thought of our own. When you think of food or your senses become stimulated by it, your body does not doubt that the experience is to follow. Your body responds in such a way that it begins the process by which to manage the very food that it anticipates receiving. It does not doubt that this will occur. How amazing is that! Your mind is just that powerful, and your body is enslaved to it. For this reason, it is evident that thoughts are creative. They are very creative. You can really work this to your advantage. However, I challenge you to be watchful of your thoughts. Give inventory to your every thought. Meditate on the pleasurable ones, and make every effort to discard the unpleasant ones. Discard the fear-filled thoughts. Ever had to perform something, but you kept entertaining the thought that you were going to mess up? When the time came for your performance you twitched, or made a slight aberrant move. You could not figure out why you had done such given that you had rehearsed this repeatedly. Well the body was just performing the way that you had prepared it to. Your fear of being unsuccessful had been terribly convincing.

Finally, Brethren, whatsoever things are true,
whatsoever things are honest, whatsoever things
are just, whatsoever things are pure, whatso-
ever things are lovely, whatsoever things are

of good report; if there be any virtue, and if
there be any praise, think on these things.
— PHILIPPIANS 4:8 KJV

The Apostle Paul was inspired to tell you those things. By now we are well aware that there are three levels by which all things take form, i.e. created. There is what you think, what you say, and what you do. The example provided here is purely cephalic, in that he is only addressing thought. Imagine if you were to advance this to the next level of creation. Oh the places you'll go!

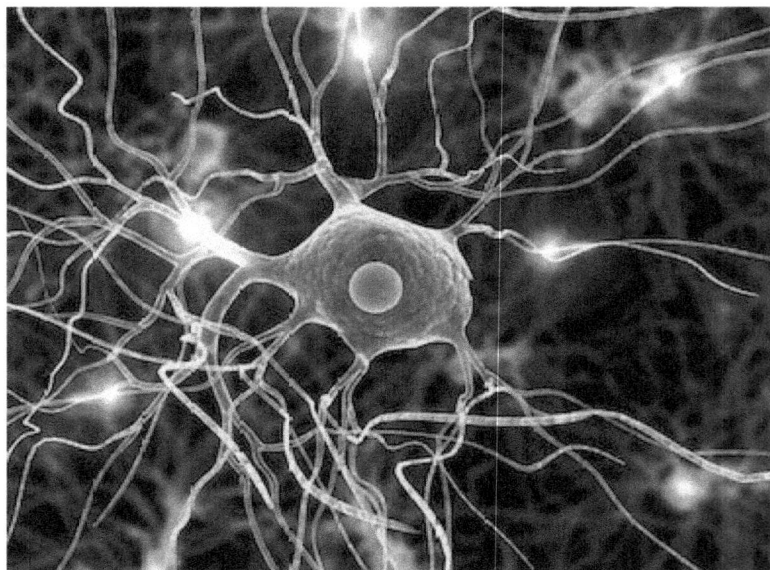

*When the Helper comes, whom I will
send to you from the Father, that is the
Spirit of truth who proceeds from the
Father, He will testify about Me.*
— JOHN 15:26 NKJV

CHAPTER 11

The Nervous System

The central nervous system is the body's ultimate regulator. It is able to integrate incoming bits of data from every part of body, rationalize it and execute a decision that will stabilize, if not amplify, the body's survival. This takes place with high fidelity. It has unfailing surveillance for every single part of the body. All of its regulatory functions are performed according to what's best for the body's survival. Not one single event can take place without first having some level of permission from this system. This, of course, is why we say that the body is a slave to the mind, in this case to the brain. It is highly sophisticated, but yet not well understood. The most advanced cells in the central nervous system are known as neurons. Neurons are the only cells in the brain that are responsible for processing information. They are made up of several parts. Let's start with dendrites. This part of the neuron is responsible for receiving information into the cell. Once this information is received, it then gets transmitted to the soma or cell body where the essential organelles of the cell are located. The soma is also the site of information processing. It is here that utilitarianism is implemented and a decision is made based on the greater good of the body; based on what amplifies the body's chances of surviving. Special note, this is far from a perfect system. The body's efforts to amplify survival in one system, could prove overtaxing in the same or another system. This no doubt may result in a state of dis-ease. Nonetheless, the soma will send its response, a message, through a narrow stalk-like channel known as the axon. The message is in the form of a chemical that will have a perfect complementary shape for the receiving cell. For the receiving cell to accept this message it must be in a recognizable form. After which, the receiving cell *must* receive the message, as it has no reasoning mind of its own. This is important. For this reason, the cells act with high fidelity, or faithfulness, and the expected response must take place. Only a *diseased* state would cause otherwise. Again, this is important. This process is ongoing all through your body all throughout the day. Now, let's parallel this to prayer. Here's why the above is so important. In each form of prayer you send out your request, or in very advanced states you make a statement (see section on prayer). It is then received by God, the ultimate central processor. He processes this request or statement and sends His response in a fashion that is irrespective of persons. Hopefully, you will be in full alignment to receive the answer to your prayer. Ideally, your ditches will have been dug and ready. Otherwise, here is where things can become complicated. Because you, unlike your cells, have a rational mind and a free will you begin to *super process* this information and act according to what you think is of greater benefit. This is a mistake. It is an art to learn to still the mind in critical times.

Let's advance this scenario. Now let's say that you are one of His most faithful servants. Recall that the message comes in a complementary form, one suited to fit you in your journey where you are right now. Secular or Christian is no matter, as this response from God can come from the next scripture that you read, it could be in the next sermon that you hear, the next book that you read, song on the radio, or movie on television. The response could even be in the next random conversation with a complete stranger. Nonetheless, it will be what we call a Rhema Word sent just for you. It will be in a perfect complementary form for you the recipient, and it will suit your situation. You will sense it because it will be designed to amplify *your* chances of survival. The key is to learn to skillfully dismiss your rational mind and receive the message. I must add that the process of answered prayer has a few more facets. This is just one of them.

There are chemical messengers within the nervous system called neurotransmitters. Their sole purpose is to faithfully deliver a message. They do not have a filtering process and thereby are incapable of altering the message in any way. They deliver the unaltered message directly to to the receiving cell, and as mentioned previously, the receiving cell must respond as it is designed to do. Nonetheless, some of the neurotransmitters may become consumed while delivering their message. As for many of them, once they deliver the message they return to where they came from. End of story. I hope you can see the correlation.

The nervous system represents our control system and is the site of information processing and decision-making. It is said to mature around the age of 50, meaning that by then all of the patterns of learning are set. Learning something "new" after the age of 50 takes place solely based on associations with a previously established pattern. So in essence, you're not learning something new, but instead you are associating new information with previous data. This is a very good thing. Yet another method of learning is called mimicry and is more commonly observed in young children. There is a certain type of neuron in the brain called a mirror neuron which helps to facilitate this. They were discovered by a group of scientists in Parma, Italy in 1992. These neurons are noted to become active not only when an individual themselves perform a certain activity, but also when someone with whom they are observing does the same. These neurons were first noted in primates. A young human brain is closer to its primate relatives. It responds to both its internal environment and external environment with very little forethought. Additionally, mimicry is a mainstay, as they are very impressionable. Ever watched a movie with a dance scene, or even listened to a friend share their story about their latest dance moves? Somewhere in your observation or listening you observe your own muscles twitch? This is why early exposure is so important in regard to cultivating skills.

Because humans have a higher functioning cortex, we are sophisticated enough to override many primitive urges, as opposed to organisms with a lower functioning cortex. However, animals with a lower functioning cortex tend to act with little to no contemplation. For this reason, they act with a high degree of fidelity. Animals act off pure instinct and make no motion to override them. We are much more complicated. Fear is the primary culprit that causes us to turn away from our natural instincts. A common subcategory of fear is the strong desire to be acclaimed and well esteemed. This is a subcategory of fear because deep at its root is the trepidation of being ill-regarded. And then there is doubt. This subcategory is a clear and evident product of a double-mind. More on this in the next chapter.

The belated Professor Morrie Schwartz is noted for constantly quoting one of W.H. Auden's most familiar lines, "Love one another or die." From birth our central nervous system must be stimulated, lest we die. This is by optimum design. Our species is born in such a helpless state that without human contact, without skin to skin, without some degree of nurturing and caring it is near impossible to survive. It is by design that we receive love. In fact, if we do not receive love one of the first systems to malfunction is the body's primary operating system, the central nervous system. The central nervous system will begin to halt development and may eventually undergo disintegration. This can range anywhere from mental delays to severe bodily impairment and even death. Think it not strange that an infant cries or screams when placed in a bouncer, but stops the moment they are consoled. It is by optimum design that we are all loved. This is why there are nurses paid to caress babies and stimulate the sensory nerves in their skin when there are no love ones available to do so. Some babies require more of this than others. Unfortunately, some children get just enough to survive and will have a much more difficult time connecting with others. This is far from an argument for autism, by the way.

It has been stated that all creation begins as a thought, from a thought comes spoken word, and from word comes deed. These are indeed the three levels of creation as stated in the book series *Conversations with God*. Someone thought of the very light fixture above your head. They likely told someone about it, or spoke of it to themselves (This is not insanity. This is creation). Thankfully the person with whom they shared it did not shut their efforts down. They then went and did something about it. They responded to the first and second order of creation. We all do this every day, all day. Ever thought about what you wanted to eat, and 30 minutes later you were enjoying it? We are truly creative. Don't dismiss the mundane. Yes, that example was on a more simple and practical scale, but trust that this can just as easily happen on a grander scale. Begin to observe your daily thoughts and before you go to bed recall the happenings of your day. As you think on the events of your day, recall the thoughts that you had that may have led to said event. Take note of them. This is a good place to start if you want to become more intentional with your creation. You will likely take notice of the less favorable ones first. Unfortunately, these situations are much easier to create if we are living a fairly "mindless" life. A life that lacks thought supplemented behavior can prove beneficial at times and dangerous at others. However, there is yet a subcategory to the creativity of thought, and that is emotion. How you feel about something carries even greater weight. Whether you have an affinity for it or an aversion to it, you will attract it if you add a dose of strong emotion to your thoughts. Here's the catch. What you will attract may not show up as you had imagined it would, but the resulting experience or feeling will be the same. If you do not desire to attract something unfavorable then identify the root of your aversion and work to transmute it. Nullify its effect. Remember the Apostle Paul says be careful for nothing.

> *Be careful for nothing; but in every thing by prayer and supplication with thanksgiving let your requests be made known unto God. And the peace of God, which passeth all understanding, shall keep your hearts and minds through Christ Jesus.*
> — PHILIPPIANS 4:6-7 KJV

Pain. Pain is caused by an incessant nerve that won't shut up, repeatedly firing off and warning you that a certain area of the body is compromised and in danger. Without adequate medical intervention it will continue until the area is healed or removed. The interpretation of this sensation can range from a bothersome itch to an overwhelming discomfort. The same can happen when God is aligning us with His truth. He will send the message in so many times, and in so many ways. It won't let up. For this reason, certain aspects of spiritual uneasiness is commonly likened to pain. When you are called by His name, or when you call His name, the words of this song will apply:

> ♫♪ "There's no shadow You won't light up,
> Mountain You won't climb up coming after
> me. There's no wall You won't kick down, lie
> You won't tear down coming after me!"♫♪
> —"RECKLESS LOVE"

CHAPTER 12

The Psyche

❧

And be not conformed to this world: but
be ye transformed by the renewing of your
mind, that ye may prove what is that good,
and acceptable, and perfect, will of God.
— ROMANS 12:2 KJV

❧

The human psyche has been described in so many ways and by various accounts. It has been said to be the mind, the consciousness, the subconsciousness, the spirit, and the soul. However, most scientists agree that it is the lot of them all. What's more, the hypothalamus of the brain is said to link them all with their physical component, the body. The hypothalamus is also a very important part of the limbic system, which processes memory. Once an experience takes place the memory of it can be processed and stored. Your soul is a collection of those memories and experiences. In this chapter we will discuss the psyche and the major influencers of it. We will also look at ways in which to alter and/or manipulate it in your favor.

The Soul

The term "soul" refers to the energy that connects you not only to others around you, but to the Greatest Soul of all. It is a part of the Great Soul, and in its purest form, it is void of any associations with name, gender, race or nationality. Because of the connection that we have with the Great Soul, we have what we commonly refer to as intuition. We can view circumstances with knowledge that we would otherwise not have. Because of our soul's connection with all that is around it, it can sense the energy of others. Have you ever been around someone whom you took an instant liking to? Or someone with whom you just couldn't get with? The soul knows all. When it is pushing information out into the conscious mind, we sense a nudge. We call this instinct. Important to note, not every instinctual behavior works for the greater good, but they work in accordance with the subconscious goals that you have set based on your life experience. In Book I of *Conversations with God*, Neale Donald Walsch writes that the soul is the sum total of every feeling that we have ever had. In the song "Te Invito," by the Colombian band Herencia, the songwriter chronicles emotional and loving moments of his life from early childhood into young adulthood. He even adds the experience of his ancestors as a part of his own life experience. He explains that all of these things make up who he is and the love that he has to offer, pure love. This depiction of collective human emotions is a beautiful example of what makes up our soul.

Have you ever recalled events of your life and began to feel the emotions surrounding those experiences? As I stated previously, emotions are energy, and according to the First Law of Thermodynamics, energy cannot be destroyed. Your soul therefore is a keeper of these experiences and emotions. Indeed, it is a compilation of memories and experiences, many of which were in place before your first breath. Whether pleasurable or scathing, some of them simply bear more weight on the psyche than others.

"The greatest pleasure is that which pleases the soul. The greatest discomfort is that which displeases the same." Dr. Cromblin

There is an innate yearning to become aware of the connection between the soul and the body. This level of awareness yields a sense of peace and serenity. Some may accomplish this through meditational practices. Others may accomplish it through religious practices. Traditional worship services may refer to this as the Holy Spirit, or the Holy Ghost. Holy because it is whole and the connection with all, with God. Some, surprisingly, may even accomplish a remarkable level of serenity through daredevil activities. In an interview with Bob Simon of *CBS's 60 Minutes*, record-breaking deep sea freediver, Tanya Streeter, reasons that she free dives into the deep because she wants to know what she's made of. She quoted the popular freediving saying, "We don't dive to look around us. We dive to look within ourselves." This practice too stems from a yearning for awareness. Regardless of the method, the act is one of mental detachment from the body. The Apostle Paul writes of this:

> *We are confident, I say, and will-*
> *ing rather to be absent from the body,*
> *and to be present with the Lord.*
> — 2 CORINTHIANS 5:8 KJV

Utterance. Language is simply an established set of utterances by populations of people and it is best understood as such. This established set of utterances affects the conveyance of ideas to bring forth communication and understanding. For example, ever watched two babies babble to each other? Their language is clearly not an established one, but yet they understand each other. They are vibrating on a certain frequency that says "give me my toy back!" The other baby understands and displays a frown of resistance. This obviously means that he rejects said suggestion. At this point the caregiver had better intervene and redirect. Often when words fail us we resort to other forms of communication. This brings up the next topic, glossolalia, or speaking in tongues. I like to call this my native language. It comprises a set of utterances that ushers in anywhere from resounding peace, to a warrior-like strength. For me, it has certainly evolved much over the years. One particular morning after having a stressful night, I woke up to a different form of glossolalia. This utterance came from a much deeper locale, yet it is one to which we all have access. Though the utterance was unintelligible to me, all the same I could perceive the message. I was in a profound state of spiritual warfare, and that which had me bound the previous night had me no more. Peace ensued. As I began to awaken I inquired within, "Lord what was that?" In spirit the understanding emerged that there was a time when it was commonplace for man to walk and talk with God in a far more direct and less filtered manner, just as we do with each other. Man was more in commune with the cosmos and could simply think, which *is* a form of prayer, a thing into existence. Since this intel was cosmically derived, she leaned not on her own understanding (Proverbs 3:5). The cosmic man was far less self-obstructive and to him availeth much. She was a great deal more *intentional* and *single-minded* that even her thoughts carried much fervor. (Psalms 12:2; James 1:8, respectively). This deeper utterance is likely most similar to Sanskrit, one of the earliest documented languages. The term Sanskrit itself means "entirely done." It is composed of established utterances based on tones, energies and frequency vibrations. It is a very conceptual language in which sentiment is often times the driving force. In this way, what is felt is spoken and what is spoken is meant. Therefore, it is apt to be used in a more deliberate manner, and for said cause is much more powerful. For this reason, many mantras are in Sanskrit.

DR. KRISTY CROMBLIN, M.D.

Now, I'm going to circle around the block with my next point, but I promise I will be back. As a believer in Christ Jesus, I have written many prayers for myself and others. I would repeat them throughout the day until I believed. Until I knew. In a sense, my prayers were mantras. Christians please stay with me. In Sanskrit, mantras always begin with the utterance "Om," symbolized as ॐ. As with many sounds of the Sanskrit language, the phonetics make for a very strong vibration. Strong vibrations are thought to harmonize and bring about pleasant vibes. Think of a massage chair, or an a capella group. Agreement is powerful. This simple word "om" represents such. It represents all that is. It is the sum total of all things. It is the Alpha and the *Omega* (great Om). It represents the gathering together of every energy, of every emotion, of light, of darkness. Yes, it even includes darkness. Though very uncomfortable, darkness represents opportunity. Here's why this is important. Love covers a multitude of errors. When love is the emotion that you choose *in the midst of darkness* then you have truly chosen the highest form of love. You have chosen perfect love. You have chosen God! Jesus teaches about this form of love in Matthew 5:44-48 KJV:

But I say unto you, Love your enemies, bless them that curse you, do good to them that hate you, and pray for them which despitefully use you, and persecute you;

That ye may be the children of your Father
which is in heaven:
for he maketh his sun to rise on the evil and on the good,
and sendeth rain on the just and on the unjust.
For if ye love them which love you, what reward have ye?
do not even the publicans the same?
And if ye salute your brethren only,
what do ye more than others? do not even the publicans so?
Be ye therefore perfect,
even as your Father which is in heaven is perfect.

There is much more to the term Om, but let us now look at an argument for possible evolution of the term. It has been postulated that om, also known as aum, evolved over time and was *super*translated into amen, a term signifying harmony and agreement. As for its origin, theologians are terribly divided such that I am at a loss to provide you with accuracy. However, as a Christian I had the pleasure of reading through a two-part commentary of the *Bhagavad Gita*, a collection of Hindu scriptures. Referred to as flesh in Christianity, the *Bhagavad Gita* does an exceptional job in explaining the ego.

Feelings

Feelings make up who you are and have been cultivated in you since birth, arguably before. These are *your* natural feelings. They become the lens by which you view life. From a happy childhood the the glass is almost always half full. From a childhood wreaked with jealousy you may find yourself at the center of destructive relationships. From a childhood of broken promises and lies you will trust no one. From a childhood filled with ridicule and mockery you will find it most difficult to open up. From a childhood inflicted with with harsh criticism self-confidence will be an uphill battle. These are natural responses from the subconscious mind and all of them can take place in adulthood as well. Yet, in all of these there is hope. He sends forever friends, teachers, mentors, and most of all His Comforter. Remember that with God all things are possible (Matthew 19:26).

When our natural feelings are challenged, be it growth or a fiery trial, we feel most uncomfortable. When we manage to push through the discomfort we do an override of our natural self. Sometimes this a very good thing, as this is the very essence of growth. However, other times it is not. These times especially present themselves in the wonder years and other crucial chapters of our lives. Without correction or realignment this can be a very unhealthy state, as the individual may repeatedly put aside their better judgement and a reprobate mind may ensue. This is a mind that will resist truth for self gain. The Apostle Paul writes of this:

> *And even as they did not like to retain*
> *God in their knowledge, God gave them*
> *over to a reprobate mind, to do those*
> *things which are not convenient...*
> — ROMANS 1:28 KJV

The human psyche has a tendency to choose heaven when filled with joy and hell while in grief. This is similar to what's known as "mood congruency" in psychology. Yet, the highest decision is always to choose heaven even when it seems to be of no avail. There will be no natural law that will prevail against you. Against such there is no law.

> *But the fruit of the spirit is love, joy, peace, longsuffering, gentleness, goodness, faith, meekness, temperance: against such there is no law.*
> — GALATIANS 5:22-23

Fear

> *...choose you this day whom ye will serve...*
> JOSHUA 24:15 KJV

Matter is anything that takes up space. A modified version of the Pauli Exclusion Principle of physics states that two objects cannot occupy the same space at the same time. You will either choose fear, or you will choose love. Either you will doubt, or you will have faith. The decision is far more simple than we make it. The rational mind is wired to add details which makes it much more complicated than it has to be. No matter, you absolutely cannot possess them concomitantly. Your mind understands this well. This is why it repeatedly goes back and forward between the two.

"Fear, an alternate state of consciousness in which survival is the ultimate goal." Dr. Cromblin

Many have noticed benefits to fear. One such benefit is partially evident by the statement, "I work better under pressure." Acute states of fear can greatly sharpen the acumen, or ability to focus, by causing a certain area of the brainstem to amplify its activity level. This area is called the reticular activating system, or RAS. When activity in the reticular activating system increases it rapidly filters out irrelevant data, utilizing only that which is pertinent to survival at that moment. The brain is wired to retain information surrounding events in which survival is perceived to be threatened, unless doing so is too debilitating. In such case those memories are suppressed.

Of course, there are the obvious disadvantages to fear. As I mentioned above, fear is an alternate state of consciousness in which survival is the ultimate goal. Let's focus on the altered state of consciousness part. Fear, and this includes stress and other forms of mental anguish, can be so overwhelming that it can cause a complete distortion of reality. This degree of stress not only distorts reality, but may also create various forms of hallucinations. In this state of fear the person is convinced that he/she is a victim of a circumstance in which they have little to no control. Orchestrated by their mind, their brain will begin to project images to justify this fervently held belief. This can be explained by the old adage that says, "From within, comes without." These distortions may include feelings of paranoia, thoughts of persecution, or the false perception of being physically attacked. This can be very dangerous. In more acute states this is what is known as a "nervous breakdown."

Doubt

As mentioned in the section on stress, fear is the beginning of stress. Fear breeds unwarranted doubt or double-mindedness. Not only is double-mindedness the act of processing two concepts in the mind at once, but it will also cause you to create multiple possible outcomes that contradict what God has already promised you, and that is that you shall have the desires of your heart. These multiple possible outcomes will most certainly lead to doubt of your initial thought, your intuition. Let me take a moment to illustrate just how tricky doubt is. Remember, it stems from double-mindedness and is nearly synonymous with it. In today's society we have every possible distraction at our fingertips. We are like babies surrounded by multiple toys, quite unsure of which one to play with next, while giving one no more than four minutes of our attention. We may go into a room with the intention to do one thing and quickly do 2-3 others prior to, or instead of. This causes us to abandon our initial thought, thereby abandoning our initial intention. Our initial thought was with purpose and was expected to yield a desired result, but it was placed aside. We do this so often until we become darn good at it. Our smartphones are making us experts at distractibility. Society encourages us in the same in by urging that we multitask. Our shifty thoughts have rewired our ability to focus and be very intent, such that when it is time to focus, and when it is time to keep our feet to the fire, our hardwire will resist every possible effort. We become distracted from our initial intent so easily. Please do not disregard this analogy. Double-mindedness and easy distractibility both labor hard against faith and strengthens doubt. How thought-provoking it is that our minute daily habits can influence our spiritual walk. Even more, we can use them as exercises to strengthen the same. So we should never negate these small opportunities. In Matthew 25:21 KJV Jesus says to you, "*Well done, thou good and faithful servant: thou hast been faithful over a few things, I will make thee ruler over many things: enter thou into the joy of the Lord.*" This scripture is obviously written within a different context. However, the statement yet holds true. Test it.

⊚⊙

Faith

"Belief is the ultimate power." Dr. Cromblin

Belief must precede faith. When you *believe* in a thing you allow it to *belive* in you. Recall that all living things must have some degree of movement about them. If what you say that you believe does not "move" you by changing your thoughts, words, or actions, then it is not alive in you. That which you believe stirs on the inside of you. It moves you. Because it is alive in you, it will lead you to take certain actions, bringing about the complementary experience. This is how you check your faith. If you haven't quite arrived there with your faith, then meet yourself where you are. As the urban saying goes, "Go for what you know!" Search for what you can believe in and work to advance your faith from there. This may take time and repetition, but *don't stop. Get it.* And remember, in this journey every round goes higher and higher. Know that there is always a better way, and there is always more. This is just one step toward building your faith.

What faith is not. Faith is not synonymous with outright dismissal. The moment that you ignore imminent or overhanging circumstances, you cast aside your opportunity to have faith. For example, if you are given an unfavorable diagnosis, do not set it aside as if it does not exist. This response does not equate to faith. Neither does having faith ignore what is blatantly obvious. Instead, in either case faith is preceded by acknowledgement of even the undesired. By faith, God will move for you in a way that is totally off of the radar. Not even His greatest seers will be able to call it.

> *But as it is written, eye hath not seen,*
> *nor ear heard, neither have entered into*
> *the heart of man, the things which God*
> *hath prepared for them that love him.*
> — 1 CORINTHIANS 2:9 KJV

The Haves and the Have Nots. Matthew 13:12 says, *"For whosoever hath, to him shall be given, and he shall have more abundance: but whosoever hath not, from him shall be taken away even that he hath."* The latter may seem more like a curse of some sort, but it is in fact more so exemplary of a state of mind. My sister often spares no expense. She enjoys quality and fashionable items, so much so that when the time comes for gift giving, be it her or her children, they always receive good gifts! I have witnessed her nearly overtaken by gifts. She reverberates an energy of *have*. Most importantly she does not thrive in the mindset of lack. Even more, she is a very generous giver. It must be stated that giving and receiving flow through the same channel. It is a destructive sense of humility to think that you are not worthy to receive good things from others, but yet you kneel in prayer requesting the same. How conflicting. The act of genuine giving should never be obstructed. At times it may need to be rerouted, but nonetheless, *always allow a person to express their good nature.* The have nots not only have little, but the little that they have gets taken away. Now even more bound by their physical experience, they remain in a perpetual mindset of *lack*. In Romans 4:17 we are inspired to overcome that which we see and put our faith into action and *"…calleth those things which be not as though they were."* Pastor Jason Warman distinguishes between the use of faith as a noun versus faith as a verb: "Faith(n) without Faith(v) is dead."

~~~

Prayer

The effectual fervent prayer of a
righteous man availeth much.
— JAMES 5:16 KJV

HEATED AIR RISES. Not only does fervent air rise like incense, but it expands while doing so. This is significant. The more heated the air becomes, the more it expands, covering ground that extends well beyond its point of origin.

Let my prayer be set forth before thee as incense...
— PSALM 141:2 KJV

My pastor regularly tells us to *make* prayer. Acts 12:5 KJV states *"...but prayer was made without ceasing..."* When we take a moment to observe, we will notice that our prayers are answered far more often than they are not. For example, if you arrived to work as you'd intended, that is a form of an answered request. Some common terms associated with prayer are request, thanksgiving, and supplication. Then there are many different modalities of prayer. On behalf of others, we can intercede, or bridge the gap between that which is seen and that which is unseen. This is called intercessory prayer. We can submit a humble petition, or repeatedly ask. This is the prayer of supplication. A subtype of the above two is called corporate prayer. This is when members of shared beliefs come together and intercede or supplicate, and is most effective when the prayer meeting is very focused and the prayer is audible by all participating. Remember, *"For where two or three are gathered together in my name, there am I in the midst of them"* (Matthew 18:20 KJV). Yet methods of prayer certainly are not limited to these few examples. And though it is symbolic of focused prayer, neither should we become fixated on the imagery of bended knee and praying hands. In fact, one of the most powerful forms of prayer is a statement. This is what is meant by dig your ditches, as referenced in 2 Kings Chapter 3. Though words and thoughts are indeed creative energy, actions require and generate more energy, thereby making a much more powerful statement of prayer. (Recall the section on E=mc^2). This is especially effective when the action is pure. In other words, all three forms of creation are in alignment. So think it, speak it, and as the urban saying goes, *"Act like you know."*

Flying High in Troubled Times. I have preached to my sons from nearly every corner of our home of how their actions make a statement about who they are, and what they are bringing about in their life. In the midst of an opportunity to choose a lesser way, challenge yourself to take the road less traveled. Remember there is always a better way. By doing this you are sending forth a statement. If strong enough you will shift your immediate environment to now accommodate this new statement of yourself. This is powerful. This is growth. This is why it is so important to extract any opportunity you can from an unfavorable circumstance. In fact, many unfavorable circumstances occur with purpose. Recall,

*Beloved, think it not strange concerning
the fiery trial which is to try you, as though
some strange thing happened unto you...*
— 1 PETER 4:12-19 KJV

Nonetheless, a prayer statement is an advanced form of prayer in which faith is now in action and you have moved past asking. You have accelerated beyond a doubtful prayer which prepares you for denial through misuse of the statement, "If it's not Your will." However, in this advanced form of prayer:

You are very clear about this scripture:
"If My people, which are called by My name.."
— 2 CHRONICLES 7:14 KJV

Your perception of this scripture is sound:
*"...no good thing will he withhold
from them that walk uprightly."*
— PSALM 84:11 KJV

You understand this scripture in absolute terms:
*"Therefore I say unto you, What things
soever ye desire, when ye pray, believe that
ye receive them, and ye shall have them."*
— MARK 11:24 KJV

Always, always, always remember that what you focus your attention on the most becomes your prayer. Prayer is merely energy in the form of a focused thought (Walsch 1998). You must use this wisely or you may inadvertently create unfavorable circumstances. This is why the Apostle Paul advises that we think on things that are of good report. Remember, E=mc².

❧

Another effective form of prayer is what I like to refer to as "visual prayer." In Philippians 4:8 KJV Paul tells us to think on those things that are of good report. *"Finally, brethren, whatsoever things are true, whatsoever things are honest, whatsoever things are just, whatsoever things are pure, whatsoever things are lovely, whatsoever things are of good report; if there be any virtue, and if there be any praise, think on these things."* In terms of prayer, visualize yourself in a desired situation. Follow this vision by making a joyful noise to reassert your vision when doubt creeps in. No, really. You should accompany this vision with a celebratory sound, or something that you like to say when you are feeling gleeful. Admittingly, it is a bit out of the box, but here we have two levels of creation working together to oppose and remove previous workings of the carnal mind. In fact, just recently our pastor said that we should always keep a prayer in our throat, almost like an irritant. Just say "ahem," as surely you don't have to make a scene while praying in the marketplace or being confronted by a coworker. Realigning God's Word in your life can be achieved simply by the sound of clearing your throat, if you so choose. If only I could retell it like he did.

Not only are there many forms of prayer, but there are many ways in which the Father answers. Sometimes our biggest mistake is to expect His answer to come in one way. Sure, there is a time and place to be explicit in your prayer and ask for specific things. However, always know that our Creator sees and knows all. Often what our soul truly desires is a certain *experience*. The specific nouns are a non-factor. The soul only cares about the experience and the resulting feeling. *"Think it not strange concerning the fiery trial which is to try you, as though some strange thing happened unto you"* (1 Peter 4:12). The experience might just be in response to your prayer. The experience that your soul leads you to worketh something greater on the inside of you. So stay the course and fight the good fight.

Every day we are subject to phenomenon that are outside of His highest order, that are apart from His optimum design. This kind often brings us to our knees. When we pray, it magnifies a focal area in our lives. For all of the above said reasons prayer, in its many forms, is a critical part of our daily living. It allows us to alter the course of events that are to befall us, or influence the same for our love ones. Prayer can also be seen as our back channel to God, in that it does not have to be made public. It IS our secret place. It can be a powerful solicitation, and can indeed shift mountain-like circumstances. It is essential because with each successive generation, there will be challenges that we, individually speaking, may not have encountered before. Our carnal mind will need to be equipped with the discernment to redirect them. For *"We wrestle not against flesh and blood, but against powers, against the rulers of the darkness of this world..."* (Ephesians 6:12 KJV). If you are wondering how you might improve your prayer life then it is important to first recognize where you are, and meet yourself there. It may suffice to start with the Lord's Prayer. Recall that in Luke 11:1 one of the disciples asked Jesus to teach them to pray. And in the book of Matthew Chapter 6 Jesus released detailed instructions regarding prayer just prior to teaching them to pray the Lord's Prayer. It is an all-inclusive prayer that is intentionally ordered such that the reverence of God precedes requests. Though it does not have to be a formal reverence, this is an important step in ensuring a divine response to your prayer.

Understand that your life is a result of His laws collaborating with your channel of truth. Your every deed soon becomes your truth. Liars soon become fools. For what you release, also a form of prayer, the same shall be returned unto you. If you habitually lie and speak rubbish, then guess what will make its rounds back to you. All fools lie. That's why they are fools.

In every moment the story of your life is being written. At any given point in time you can alter your course. There are innumerable alternate endings and not one person is permitted to give you solid prophecy of such. For some of you that may be a relieving thought. Yes, according to 1 Corinthians 2:10, there are spiritually inclined individuals who are permitted to see beyond the present time with near pristine accuracy, but not even they can foresee all. Their gift is limited to only what is revealed. How blessed is it when a divine stealth-like interruption alters the sequence of events to yield a blessed result! As previously referenced, "...*Eye hath not seen, nor ear heard, neither have entered into the heart of man, the things which God hath prepared for them that love him*" (1 Corinthians 2:9 KJV). In medicine we call this a miracle.

One of my hardest lessons was to learn that often what I asked for God would instead send me the opportunity to get it. It's like your child asking you for a new game system. You say "yes." The child then comes back the next day and asks when are you going to purchase it. You say "Well, I spoke to the neighbor and she says that you can get started on her yard right away!" Listen, I cannot emphasize enough that shortly after your prayer follows the opportunity. Unfortunately, all too often these opportunities are acknowledged for what they were in hindsight. In another example, you may feel the urge to contact someone with whom you have not spoken with in some time. From that conversation comes an opportunity for your long awaited for prayer to be answered. This just happened to me a short while ago. Don't dismiss the little voice. Don't overlook the unction. Start with the menial things and before you know it you've mastered it. Recall in Matthew 25:23, where Jesus reminds us of the reward in honoring the small things. Let us now study the Lord's prayer. God gives us the opportunity to allow His will to be done. He gives us the opportunity to receive our daily bread, be it physical bread or manna from heaven. He gives us opportunities to both be forgiven and to forgive. In all of these things there exists an opportunity for us to do something. The Great Book is filled with Word that will make us strong against temptation and through prayer we will be delivered from the hands of evil.

> *After this manner therefore pray ye:*
> *Our Father which art in heaven,*
> *Hallowed be thy name.*
> *Thy kingdom come, Thy will be done*
> *in earth, as it is in heaven.*
> *Give us this day our daily bread.*
> *And forgive us our debts, as*
> *we forgive our debtors.*
> *And lead us not into tempta-*
> *tion, but deliver us from evil:*
> *For thine is the kingdom, and the*
> *power, and the glory, for ever.*
> *Amen.*
> MATTHEW 6:9-13 KJV

There is always a better way and there is so much more that God has for His people. Jesus said that the Kingdom of Heaven is at hand. Prayer opens it up. No matter the style of prayer, give it true meaning and focused attention. Be very present in your thoughts and other forms of communication with God. When you are finished telling Him your side of the story, be open for His afterwards. Remain open to His version of how your journey might advance.

Sin

Sin can be a dreadful word. The oversimplified definition of it is wrongdoing. A less judgemental view of sin is to miss the mark, or not quite get there. However, the meaning of sin is so much more vast and expandable. Moving away from the judgement aspect of sin, it simply means to think, speak, or act in a way that is outside of His highest will and does not lead to that heavenly state of being. That is it. And yes, as sure as you are an incarnate on earth you are subject to "sinning" throughout the day, but we are not without help. Know this, every soul has the potential to respond to goodness and we all yearn to experience that heavenly place. Though there are many routes to this place, some choose a convoluted path. Some choose a more narrow and direct path. Nonetheless, sin is what keeps us off the narrow and direct path, and there are many. These offsets can range from what we think, to what we do. No matter the offset, it is yet a deterrent from the great path. However, Jesus came to give us hope. Recall that in Jesus's very first sermon He told the people of Galilee, *"Repent: for the Kingdom of Heaven is at hand"* (Matthew 4:17 KJV). God has inspired many contemporary authors to write that the Kingdom of Heaven is "nowhere," understood as "nowhere." All things that you stand in the need of and all things that you desire are right here, right now. You just need the revelation of it. This means that there is no getting "there." So if fear, disbelief, or your ego are what's causing you to miss the mark, then change your disbelief right here, right now. If fear is what's causing you to miss the mark, begin to trust in His Word right here, right now. Remember, you cannot serve two masters. Either trust Him, or go your way in fear. These two examples support His call to "repent." So you see, there is no *getting there* to some distant location or some forever moving goalpost. The mark is right here. For most people getting "there" depends on some huge event they hope will take place in the future. This belief is far from scriptural. This idea also takes the responsibility off of you the believer, to act right now. Note, responsible is simply a term that means: to respond accordingly to the need at hand. Therefore, taking the responsibility off of yourself makes *you* less responsive, or irresponsible. Be more responsive to what you need and desire by acting *now*. The kingdom of heaven *is* at hand.

∽⊙⊙∼

You are Powerful!

Jesus dissolved fear. Jesus dissolved heartache. Jesus dissolved anxiety. Jesus dissolved depression. Jesus dissolved sorrow. Jesus dissolved illness. Jesus even dissolved death. Such that in the midst of *your* fear, heartache, anxiety, depression, sorrow, illness and death you can now call forth assurance, joy, peace, serenity, well-being, and even life.

> *...and greater works than these shall he*
> *do; because I go unto my Father.*
> — JOHN 14:12 KJV

Whatever unfavorable experience you may be enduring, attempt to experience the opposite. Every time the thought of misery arises interrupt that thought with a celebrant utterance and a pleasant visual. Yes, of course you want to keep this as private as possible as it may appear that you are not well. Cancel out the thought that is not of His optimum design for your life. In no time you will find that you have transcended your current situation. You have dissolved it.

In Psalm 82:6, David is inspired to write that we are all gods and prodigy of the most High God. In John 10:34, Jesus made a reference to this very scripture. I once had a student who counseled with me regarding her health. She came to me in frustration that she had to pay a large sum of money for a doctor's visit and prophylactic medication for an anticipated urinary tract infection (UTI). She mentioned that she indeed did get the UTI as they had expected, but the prophylactic antibiotic did not work. I asked her a series of questions, but we weren't meeting with much resolve, as she was very frustrated at having had spent a large sum of money for her visit and medication. She then expressed with agitation, "and the one time I actually take the medicine it didn't work. That is why I never take medicine." I said, "There it is! That is why it did not work. You had already preconditioned the outcome." Often we have to be reminded of just how powerful we are in both the mundane and the major. As I have mentioned before, many are our answered prayers. If you broaden your understanding of prayer it becomes much more clear that her statement of prayer was actualized.

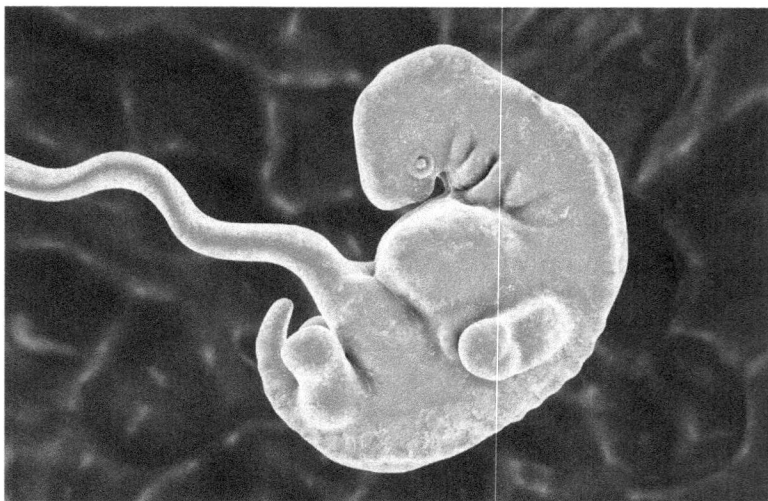

Before I formed you in the womb I knew you;
Before you were born I sanctified you;
— Jeremiah 1:5 NKJV

CHAPTER 13

Reproduction

There are 23 pairs of chromosomes. 22 pairs of those chromosomes are autosomal, meaning that they have the blueprint for all mechanisms of the body except for the reproductive system. The last set of chromosomes is the sex chromosomes. Of course, the genes on this set are more active in the cells concentrated in the perineal and genital areas. This area only makes up about 1% of the body's total surface area, *regardless of who you are.* Densely packed with sensitive nerve endings, that 1% is the driving force behind many, if not most, human interactions. Not only that, it is the major facilitator in the gift of life. All things considered, that makes the genitalia pretty powerful. But we already knew that. As mentioned above, there is only one set of chromosomes that is primarily responsible for the genitalia. Though the degree of gene expression may be influenced by multiple factors, it is on this set of chromosomes where the males are separated from the females, thereby playing an essential role in gender identity and human sexuality. There is more to be said of both the former and the latter, but for now may it be boldly noted that in His presence neither of them hold any importance, whatsoever. You are a soul. And perhaps one of the most liberating scriptures for anyone feeling the pains of gender confinement is Galatians 3:28 KJV *"There is neither Jew nor Greek, there is neither bond nor free, there is neither male nor female: for ye are all one in Christ Jesus."* In your purest form and in your most heavenly state you are simply a soul, an extension of Him, and nothing else matters.

The zygote. You got your start as a one-celled organism immediately following the union of the egg cell carrying your mother's lineage and the sperm cell carrying your father's lineage. The zygote then underwent a number of cell divisions, eventually producing new cells that would do the same. As the zygote undergoes numerous cell divisions it eventually becomes an embryo and on to a fetus, various stages of evolvement can be observed. In fact, during its embryonic stage it takes on a very similar appearance to many lower level animals during the same stage. Could 40 weeks of human gestation be telling of the ever evolving human race as a whole? Can this be an example of the soul's journey? The process of cell division extends beyond birth, slowing down notably in early adulthood, and on to death. From conception onward, you have gone through numerous changes. You still are. It will not stop. However, as an implied rule we refer to these changes as development in the ages prior to 25 years, and aging thereafter.

See that you do not despise one of these little ones. For I tell you that their angels in heaven always see the face of my Father in Heaven.

— MATTHEW 18:10 NIV

CHAPTER 14

Growth and Development

⌒⊙⊙⌒

...Let the little children come to me,
and do not hinder them, for the kingdom
of heaven belongs to such as these.
— MATTHEW 19:14 NIV

⌒⊙⊙⌒

Child Psychology

*S*oul. It is so important that children learn that they are a
soul foremost and above all else. They should learn that
they are regarded as a loved and loving being before
emphasizing any other confining roles. It is then and only
then should other social identifiers be added: gender, nationality, race, talents etc. This is not necessarily accomplished

through lecturing the child, but instead experience, which may require the parents and/or guardians to first be aware of the same themselves. *"For every tree is known by its own fruit"* (Luke 6:44 NKJV).

Perception. It's well known that children understand the world through perception. With that said, cause them to perceive goodness. Cultivate comfort and happiness in a child from birth such that it becomes commonplace. It becomes her comfort zone. As the child matures he will be more inclined to make decisions that will lead him back to that familiar place. This sets the stage for building overall confidence. That's half the battle. Cultivating comfort and happiness also enhances a child's adaptability and greatly reduces incidences of depression. For in our darkest hour we always seek to find that place of comfort familiarity. Thereby be full of care when introducing fear, or the notion of fear, to such young minds, lest you will see that decision-making will stem from a place of fear, as opposed to the pursuit of happiness. This is very important. Additionally, young minds should also be impressed by the notion that promises exist and that they can be kept. This too is very important. Otherwise, it will be difficult for them to conceive God's promises. Start by making small promises that you can be certain to keep. By building this concept you will construct a healthy-minded adult who will not only be cognizant of a promise being actualized, but will likely be convicted to produce the same. There will come a time in every adult's life when having a healthy concept of a fulfilled promise will be crucial.

*...(elders) nor as being lords over those entrusted
to you, but being examples to the flock.*
— 1 PETER 5:3 NKJV

Child Rearing. In the above scripture, Peter is referencing expectations for leaders and their relationship with those entrusted to them. By this same token we can address a very important aspect of parent-child relationships. As a parent you blaze the path. You are the guide through that path and beyond. In other words, collect wisdom from your mistakes. Then be present and share your wisdom. Most importantly, *demonstrate* the necessary acts to steer your offspring. Children model experienced behavior so it is crucial for parents to exemplify that which they wish to see in their children. It is critical for this period in their lives to be properly guided. However, this may require a great deal more than conventional wisdom. Each child is different, encompassing different problem-solving skills. Some may cry to escape a problem; some may lie (Yes, lying is a problem-solving skill.), and some may act out physically. No matter their skill set, the guiding adult is pressed to train them to remain within the confines of the law and social norms of society, all the while not being obstructive to who they are. This can be tricky, as some laws need reevaluation and some social norms should be challenged. Again, this may require more than conventional wisdom. You have the access.

Know Your Child. Many behavioral issues and issues of discord can be traced back to the acts of, often times, well-meaning parents. This can be as simple as a bread-winning parent working a double shift on the day that bullying at school has reached its peak. These parents have either placed their child in a position that they do not want to be in, or have failed to place their child in a position that they *needed* to be in. Of course, either of the two will be a key factor in the development of the child's disposition, or natural attitude. I call this childhood dispositioning. Take the time during early childhood to observe and understand your child's mannerism. If your child is highly affectionate, then be careful not to shun them away when they ask for it. If your child asks serial questions, then your job is to position them such that knowledge pours in. If you've got a very active child, or a muscular child then it is essential to keep them moving. In all of these the genes are just expressing themselves. Allow them. To do otherwise is to obstruct them, or to get in the way of something that wants to be externally pressed, or expressed. To obstruct something that wants to be expressed is to create frustration. Incidentally, many adults among us have this sort of chronic background frustration and have yet to learn how to deal with it. If the child is not properly coached through these stages a fixation will likely ensue and carry over into adulthood. Nonetheless, it is up to the parent to allow expression, but harness it in such a way as not to be a threat to their freedom or survival. Aside from the most obvious parental duties, food, shelter, safety, this is the true essence of parenting.

Overgeneralization. The simple mind generalizes quickly, and with no opposing thought. This is commonly seen in very young children. For example, a toddler may see a four-legged animal and call it a "pup pup" when it may actually be a kitten. As their brain develops so should they. This can be perfected through exposure. Parents should enhance their ability to apply discriminative thought by training them to identify the nuances of very similar objects and be able to distinguish one from the other. This certainly has its place. Now let's advance this idea. Say there is someone who did not advance far past the stage of generalization. A common way that this is revealed is through race relations. To encounter someone who has truly escaped from the mental confinements of racial classifications is a treasure and a rare find, so much so that anyone making strides away from it should be commended. With racial classifications comes the act of overgeneralization and prejudgement, or prejudice. This is a very broad and wide topic and not every committed act should be demonized. Nonetheless, regardless of the reasoning, it is primitive and we should all work to minimize it. Bear in mind, the most open-minded individual understands even the most narrow-minded of those among them.

"You're only as open-minded as the closed-minded person with whom you cannot understand." Dr. Cromblin

For you are all sons of God through faith in Christ Jesus.
GALATIANS 3:26 NKJV

Genotype XY:
Let the Boys be Boys

The Testosterone Surge. With an increasingly hearty appetite, acne across his forehead, and random bouts of unjustified aggression, a male child's behavior will change. He may exhibit more intolerance, and/or territorial behavior. The more muscular the build the more likely the aggression will be expressed in a physical nature. The less muscular, the more verbal, or as he gets older the more likely he is to make use of tools to carry out his aggression. In extreme cases when this child feels most unheard, or when he feels that his voice is falling on deaf ears, he may resort to using objects as an alternative means of expression. These are difficult times for both the child and the parents, and in extreme cases, dangerous as well. It is a critical crossroads for him.

Now, consider a male child who has been nurtured by his mother or other female figure. Because of their bond, he takes great joy in making her proud. As with all children, he will undergo very essential developmental stages. According to Kohlberg's Cognitive-Developmental Theory, one of the three stages of gender development is the gender identity stage. This is the first stage and occurs at, or around, age two. At this point, the child understands that they are male or female and that other people are categorized this way as well. Both internal and external influences will be key factors both before and after this stage. Some psychologist argue that this stage may occur even sooner, but because of language limitations the child may not be able to express it. Then there is puberty. In this child something seemingly new is on the rise, and can be *very* confusing. With a surge in hormones, namely testosterone, his feelings, and consequently his outlook, begin to change. Does he go on to make the most forceful ally he knows proud and continue to take up her ways? Or does he pull away from her and go his separate way? The more *dominant* and influential the female figure, the more likely that he will choose the former. When we study gene expression we see that we have the ability to either up-regulate a gene or down-regulate it. In this case, it seems that the dominant female figure, particularly if she is detailed-oriented, near castrates the male by upregulating her X chromosome and consequently down regulating his Y chromosome. This is the popular argument of nature vs nurture in psychology. This dominant feminine figure nurtures him and/or governs him such that the estrogen suppressive traits of the Y chromosome are no longer effective. The genes on the Y chromosome have an indirect estrogen suppressive effect simply by doing what they do naturally, causing the production and release of testosterone. The persistent presence of a dominant female figure has a way of influencing, or nurturing his X chromosome, consequently downregulating the genes on the opposing Y chromosome. These genetic changes may take place very early on and will most definitely become externally pressed, or expressed. In fact, there have been multiple studies to show that there is now evidence of similarities in both the brain structure and function of a heterosexual female and that of a homosexual male. These genetic alterations may even be underway before the child has understood their gender role, and so the child will say "I was born this way." In a sense, they are not far from the truth at all.

Please note, this in no way explains every circumstance, but it certainly makes the case for many.

Now take a child that takes joy in making his father proud. One that has always stayed out of trouble, and has been praised by many. All of a sudden he now becomes angry about the slightest of things. His grades are dropping in school, and he is constantly getting into trouble. With his father's guidance, at some point he begins to understand that in order to remain within the confines of society, a bit of this aggression must be contained. In some instances the young man is able to work through his aggression until he reaches the age of understanding. In some cases, he is not.

In both of the examples above, a form of suppression takes place. This is obstruction. Know this: the inner man always yearns to be expressed. To hinder such creates a sense of frustration, which will later cause a random release or lead to depression. As a general rule in medicine, anything that is meant to flow should always remain in flux. For obstruction fosters destruction. However, on the parents' part this flux may need guidance and/ or occasional rerouting. No matter, a male must decide his path. This is the crossroads that every man has taken, and every male child must take. It cannot be avoided. Even more, it is during this time that much is born, both the favorable and the unfavorable. Failure to cope with these changes can prove deleterious. Recall the section on pain. Sometimes the pain, or spiritual uneasiness, can be quite tormenting and not so easily relieved. This can be particularly concerning in young children and teenagers, as they have not fully grasped the concept of a better tomorrow.

And then there is the case of protective love. All children, no matter the gender, cling toward the one with whom provides protection whether it be either a parent, a grandparent, an older sibling, or a distant relative. A special bond will be formed between that one who protects, and defends and that one who is on the receiving end of the same.

A grandchild is the mark of life renewed and a crown to the aged.
To my Kaerah Eva

Even to your old age, I am He,
And even to gray hairs I will carry you!
— Isaiah 46:4 NKJV

CHAPTER 15

Glory Years

This chapter was written from one of the most ideal places, Venice, Florida. Venice is a retirement community renowned for its vibrance and its hospitality toward older adults. It's not surprising to hear live bands and see people dancing at 4:00 in the afternoon, on a Wednesday. Neither is it uncommon to find 80-year-olds bike-riding and active in community sports like tennis and baseball. I absolutely love it. Here recreational activity is encouraged. Since being here, I have received some very helpful tips on aging. Of all, the most reverberated advice is to stay active and always have fun. Another very common piece of advice is to make many friends. I have encountered some of the most lively older adults with some of the best life stories here in Venice. However, not all of them share the same views regarding aging. A few have advised me that whatever I do "don't get old." Needless to say, I won't be taking that advice. One friend shared his story with me of how he would regularly ask God, "Why are you keeping me here.

I am ready to go." He said that the very next thought was one that reminded him of the number of people he prays for every day. He went on to detail his prayer routine. It encouraged him, as sometimes we just want to be assured that our journey here is not in vain and that it has served a higher purpose. Another friend said that the worst part about getting older, aside from a decline in bodily functions, is watching your loved ones and friends die before you. She provided several examples of when she experienced this. I asked her what helps her to get through it. What are the highlights of her day? She replied that when love ones call or visit it helps her to look forward to another day. Yet another friend with macular degeneration who needed my help said that she never thought that she would be so decrepit in old age. I intercepted that thought by telling her that "life has a way of reminding us that we all need each other." My children's babysitter would often advise that young people should always have an older person with whom they can call. I challenge you to do the same. Seek their counsel. Listen to their stories. Reinforce their memory. Befriend them. *Walk them home.*

A few months ago, my pastor responded to a death in the church family by preaching a very moving sermon entitled, "When Over There Starts Looking Better Than Over Here," derived from 2 Corinthians 4:8-18. He spoke of loved ones who had already made their great return, and how joyous both sides would be to see each other again. He stated that as the body ages and becomes more tired, that for some, the vision of crossing over becomes stronger and stronger. Giving numerous examples of chronic illnesses, he likened the dysfunctional body to a cracked pot, stating "but inside of this cracked pot is an untouched treasure that is more valuable than anything seen."

> *Therefore we do not lose heart. Though out-*
> *wardly we are wasting away, yet inwardly we*
> *are being renewed day by day. For our light*
> *and momentary troubles are achieving for*
> *us an eternal glory that far outweighs them*
> *all. So we fix our eyes not on what is seen,*
> *but on what is unseen, since what is seen is*
> *temporary, but what is unseen is eternal.*
> — 2 CORINTHIANS 4:16-18, NIV.

CHAPTER 16

Death

*Brothers and sisters, we do not want you
to be uninformed about those who sleep
in death, so that you do not grieve like the
rest of mankind, who have no hope.*
— 1 THESSALONIANS 4:13 (NIV)

*T*he Great Return. Recapping on the sermon, "When Over There Starts Looking Better Than Over Here," when a soul has decided to make the great return there is very little that anyone else can do to alter this course. Two or three can gather, but it will be to little or no avail. This is a very sacred moment in which another promise is at work. "...and He shall give you the desires of your heart" (Psalm 37:4 NKJV). This is the point where it is between her and her maker, between you and God. This decision can come about rapidly in some cases, or unbeknownst to love ones, can be a long time coming in others. In fact, on the day that the sermon was preached, there was a member in the congregation who heard the message differently from the rest. He later admitted that his focus was on the title of the sermon and seeing his loved ones again. After years of suffering from chronic illnesses and carrying around a body that could no longer perform the way that he needed it to, he found solace in the sermon. He made his great return not long afterwards. The ultimate decision will always be yours above all else.

Energy is neither created or destroyed. Recently my hometown suffered a major loss, a murder-suicide. In times, past events like these made national news, no matter the state. Now they seem to be way too commonplace. As I sit and think of my former schoolmates, I think of a mother whose inner energy was forcibly severed from its carnal attachment. She can no longer smell. She can no longer taste. She is not able to appreciate the touch of her children. There are no sensory nerves alive to report it, and no central nervous system by which to process it. Though she is indeed witnessing the tears of her children and love ones, but she is no longer privileged to produce the same. I think of a father whose inner energy had suffered an enormous amount of grief and conflict. So much so that the boundaries between life and death became far less distinct, making death appear to be the better option. Remember, energy is neither created or destroyed. Though limited in regards to his physical form, his inner energy yet thrives. Her inner energy will never ever cease to exist. As I always tell my students, sometimes to understand what something is, you have to understand what it is not. This part is not completely about death, but about *Life* as well. What they can no longer do, we can, and we must.

Regularly we go through life completing activities of daily living with no conscious thought. However, genuine living means that you are not so consumed by past events or future upcomings, but instead you are aware of your body and what you are actually sensing or feeling at the present time. For example, wiggle your third toe on your right foot. It is highly unlikely that you are aware of at any point throughout your typical day, but such a brief moment of presence can snatch your attention off of the concerns of tomorrow. Yes, a peculiar example for sure, but yet it is true. All too often we go through the motions of life and miss the simple pleasures of actually living, actually feeling. It is amazing how such a simple practice can bridge the gap between a monotonous life filled with what we perceive as unanswered prayers, into a state of peace and blissfulness. Now, can you think of a time when it seemed that you could feel every touch and sense every sensation about you? And would you also say that during those times you *felt more alive*? Good. It's not that hard after all. That is no coincidence.

This morning as I was preparing to write I saw a huge spider in my bedroom. In as much as I value life in many forms, I immediately began to see this spider as a much lower form of life that would in some way threaten my survival. My ultimate goal was to disable it enough to get it out of the house, but I was not shying away from the idea of killing it either. To make this depiction of the value of life more much practical, let me just add that this is the beginning of many of our wrongful killings. One person feels threatened by another in which they have deemed as a "lowlife," "a piece of trash" because they obviously do not share the same values. If a confrontation ensues that one who has esteemed herself above the other will argue ferociously that she was within her right. This may even involve peculiar details that can not be validated. In the case of misused firearms, imagine that the two souls involved, the aggressor and the subject of aggression, are both a part of the same body. They are both a part of the *One Soul*. Now in this moment both of the bodily components are operating outside of their optimal capacity, in that they are both driven by an energy that is far from their highest Self, ie. rage, hurt, fear. In simplest terms, they are both hurting. This can have grave consequences. Which part of the body do you render aid to first? In your little prayer box who should you focus your prayers on the most? Your first thought may be the one being harmed, the one who is about to die unjustifiably; the victim, or their family. No. In medicine if one part of the body is creating a disease state in another part of the body, you correct the culprit first. In this way, the now corrected one will do harm no more. If not healed all together, the disease process will consequently halt in the other part of the body. That is why if there was such a thing as order of prayer, you would pray for this one first. Indeed this would be most difficult for some, but this would be doing the greatest good. This is utilitarianism. Always remember, we are all in this together. In fact, much of what we experience in this journey emanates from our intrinsic, though not always agreeable, partnership with each other.

Some time ago, I was working up one of my patients who had a host of health problems. Most of his health issues were acquired through health-hazard decisions that he had made in the decades prior. He constantly complained of them. He had advice for younger people on how to age better than he had himself. However, as the exchange continued, or should I say digressed, current events worked their way into the conversation. He commenced to advise me on not so well-known ways to own a firearm without a license. All of this was fine until he began to counsel me on how to get away with murder. Immediately, I resolved that the root cause of his health problems were not from his previous health hazard decisions alone, but instead stemmed from his lack of value for life, human life in particular. Unfortunately, he is far from alone. By many accounts, domesticated animals are now regarded much higher than our fellow humans who, to some, have fallen from grace.

But be ye reminded of this:

"If a man say, I love God, and hateth his brother, he is a liar: for he that loveth not his brother whom he hath seen, how can he love God whom he hath not seen? And this commandment have we from him, That he who loveth God love his brother also."

— 1 JOHN 4:21-22

And never forget this:

"...God is love; and he that dwelleth in love dwelleth in God, and God in him."

— 1 JOHN 4:16

To give light to them that sit in darkness and in the shadow of death, to guide our feet into the way of peace.
— LUKE 1:79 KJV

CHAPTER 17

Spiritual Application

In Him was life; and the life
was the light of men.
— JOHN 1:4 KJV

N ot one part of your true being is through happenstance. You were made with intention. You are part of a greater strategy. So do not forgo the essence of your true nature. Find your way back to that place where it was just you and Him, and you knew Him. Remembering that God is in all and is all, there is no place that you can go that love can not reach you. The author of *All the Way to Heaven*, Elizabeth Sherrill, chronicles her journey to Christ while juggling the duties of motherhood, wife, etc. She states that God spoke to her in a time of distress saying, "I am in the peas on the floor." How inspirational is that! Just as He spoke to her, He speaks to you. So do not dismiss that random profound thought that seems to occupy its very own space. Be aware of the thought that made everything make sense. Consider that very clear thought that is so indisputably worded such that you are at a loss to counter it. Do not shrug off the random, but timely, statement that your little one just made. He is speaking to you. You are just that important.

Knowing that we can still be in direct communion with Him gives us hope. Knowing that there are promises and prayers stored up in high places is encouraging. Yet there will be experiences that challenge us, some to the brink. There will be love ones who often through their own journey to find themselves, seemingly hurt us. And there will be outright enemies. However, it is no matter. The promise is not that you will be free of strife and that no weapon would form against you once you are in His Kingdom. For as sure as you are on this side of the firmament you are subject to everything that nature and humanity has to offer. Instead, He promised that it would not prosper. Keep this promise close to heart during these times. Never stop growing and getting better each day. Let your good become better, and your better your best.

Just as an oak tree started from a seed, so can you. Meet yourself where you are and never stop advancing. Do not miss the small opportunities for growth, or the value rendering a small kind gesture. Delight yourself in even the most wee opportunities to be better. They matter. For it is in the smallest things that your salvation lies.

...Well done, thou good and faithful ser-
vant: thou hast been faithful over a few

things, I will make thee ruler over many
things: enter thou into the joy of thy Lord.
— MATTHEW 25:21 KJV

This scripture has been referenced several times throughout
the book already. The parable tells of three servants to which
all were given a share of talents or gifts. Those who used their
gifts were given more. He who didn't, that one that he had was
taken. Anytime you use your gift you *encourage, or* strengthen
it. Gifts are simply aspects of a person in which their connection with God, the Divine, is more potent and concentrated.
No matter how minute it may seem, absolutely never discount
your gift. That little thing that you are good at: Work it! Work
it! Work it! Take baby steps. Don't miss an opportunity. No
matter how small. Act as soon as He gives you the inspiration,
lest your rational self will dismiss it. Once you learn to act
quickly on your intuition you will become better and better
at it. I can not emphasize it enough, do not dismiss the small
victories. It is true, the more you know the more you grow.

Ignorance is lost through the acceptance of the revelation of
knowledge. For not only is ignorance lost, but deliverance is
gained. This is growth. Knowledge is constantly being revealed
around us, but less often is it received. Not all that is noted here
will be well received, but remember truth will always nudge us,
particularly if we sincerely desire it. As the old and contemporary adages go, "When the student is ready the teacher will
appear. When the student is truly ready the teacher will disappear." When you take serious inquiry of truth He will shift

planets and move the stars to send it to you. Your teacher of truth may come in the form of a child, or an animal, or a true mentor herself. When you have mastered the journey of truth, you will become the teacher.

We have journeyed through the creation of man from spoken Word alone, to her actualization and beyond. To understand that we are made in His image, it would serve us well to study and seek a deeper understanding of His Word. In this, prayer and meditation are key. But for a more profound understanding of Him we may be charged with truly putting aside some things.

> *This kind can come forth by noth-*
> *ing, but by prayer and fasting.*
> — MARK 9:29 KJV

We have only covered the tip of the iceberg when it comes to such, but it is a start. It is my hope that this book has sustained some, refined others and retrieved most. In a time when Christianity is mocked by Hollywood, I cannot emphasize it enough, do not give up on God. Do not give up on the assembly of kindred spirits for the benefit of your growth. For every color of personality, He has raised up several leaders who have said "Yes" just for the sake of *your soul.* Let it not be all for naught. Find your fit under an anointed leader or leadership that will assist in your growth. Use the prayer tools here to help you define and fortify your prayer life. You will need it. Through prayer and meditation (silent time), you will grow to appreciate that His Word *is* indeed evidence that stands beyond any reasonable doubt. Effectively minister these truths to others each time the opportunity presents. Labor for souls. For *"The harvest truly is great, but the labourers are few"* (Luke 10:2 KJV). Do not get weary in well-doing. Yet take time for yourself to enjoy life. Intently enjoy the company of family and friends, such that your grief is minimal when they decide to make their great return. Be recreational. And lastly, do not forgo your sabbath. Take mental breaks and time away from the hustle and bustle of life. Do this often. In all of these things, it is my hope that you will evolve such that your glory years will be just that.

I pray that I have done the message in this compendium its due diligence.

(end)

He that hath ears to hear, let him hear.
— MATTHEW 11:15 KJV

REFERENCES AND RESOURCES

Note: No one person mentioned in this book validates every statement that has been made.

https://www.kristycromblin.com

The Holy Bible: King James Version (KJV)

The Holy Bible: New King James Version (NKJV), Thomas Nelson (1982)

The Holy Bible: New International Version (NIV), Zondervan (2011)

Peterson, Eugene H. The Message: The Bible in Contemporary Language (MSG), (2002)

Albom, Mitch. *Tuesdays with Morrie: An old Man, a Young Man, and Life's Greatest Lesson*. New York, NY: Doubleday, 1997.

Asbury, Cory, C. Culver, and R. Jackson. *Reckless Love*. Bethel Music Publishing, 2017.

Auden, W.H. *Another Time:* "September 1, 1939." New York: Random House, 1940.

Birts, Mark E., N. Martinelli. Fat Larry's Band. *Act Like You Know*. Unidisc Music, Inc., 1982.

Begner, Vasquez. Herencia de Timbiqui. *Te Invito*. Bombo Records, 2015.

CBS 60 Minutes with Bob Simon. "Free Diving." Aired January 13, 2013. https://www.cbsnews.com/news/death-defying-free-dives-push-boundaries/

Conner, Steve. "The Cell Atlas: Biology's Next Mega Project Will Find Out What We're Really Made of." *MIT Technical Review*, March-April 2017: 58-61.

Cromblin, William E. "Archived Sermon Notes." Open Door Christian Faith Worship Center (ODCF), Montgomery, AL., 2006-2018. https://www.facebook.com/profile.php?id=100008614756202

Jammer, Max. *Einstein and Religion: Physics and Theology*. Princeton, NJ: Princeton University Press, 1999.

"Kohlberg's Cognitive Developmental Theory of Gender." ScienceAid, scienceaid.net/psychology/gender/cognitive.html Accessed 17 Jan 2019.

Mader, Sylvia S. and Michael Windelspecht. *Essentials of Biology*. Fourth Edition. New York, NY: McGraw-Hill Education, 2015

Patton, K., and Gary Thibodeau. *Anatomy & Physiology.* Ninth Edition. St. Louis, MO: Elsevier, 2016.

Ridenour, Fritz. So What's the Difference. Bloomington, MN: Bethany House Publishers, 2001

Schucman, Helen. *A Course in Miracles: Combined Volume.* Third Edition. Valley, CA: Foundation for Inner Peace, 2007

Sherrill, Elizabeth. *All the Way to Heaven: A Surprising Faith Journey.* Grand Rapids, MI: Revell, 2002.

Smith, Sandra Lee. "Heart Period Variability of Intubated Very-Low-Birth-Weight Infants During Incubation Care and Maternal Holding." *American Journal of Critical Care*, Jan 2003: 54-63.

Thomas, Julian. *Think, Plan, and Succeed B.I.G. (by Involving God): Simple Ways to Achieve Uncommon Success in Life.* Christian Faith Publishing, 2016. http://www.drjulianthomas.com

Oerter, Robert. *The Theory of Almost Everything: The Standard Model, the Unsung Triumph of Modern Physics.* New York: Pearson Education, 2006.

Tyson, Neil Degrasse. *Astrophysics for People in a Hurry.* New York: W.W. Norton & Company, 2017.

Walsch, Neale Donald. *Conversations with God: An Uncommon Dialogue.* Book 1. New York, NY: G.P. Putnam's Sons, 1995.

Walsch, Neale Donald. *Conversations with God: An Uncommon Dialogue.* Books 2 and 3. Newburyport, MA: Hampton Roads Publishing Company, 1997,1998.

Warman, Jason. Coastlife Church. Venice, Florida. https://mycoastlifechurch.com

Webster, Shaemun C. School of Ministry Excellence (SOME) Montgomery Campus. Tower of Prayer Church, Leeds, AL. https://www.facebook.com/thetowerofprayer/

Though it may be referenced in an academic setting, this book is meant for a popular audience.

Note: No one person mentioned in this book validates every statement that has been made.

MORE GRATITUDE

"It will be an inspiration." -Thank you Dr. Julian Thomas for speaking the Word that urged me to move forward with this work.

I thank my parents for rearing me with space and freedom to be myself. I can not think of one time when they did otherwise. I thank them for causing me to experience love and safety in this world. Thank you Dad for making me know that I have a voice. I thank you for being my pastor and delivering sermons that pulled me out of the pits of hell. Thank you Mom for your delightful and joyous spirit that spread throughout our home. And thank you for cultivating creativity in me.

I truly love and thank you both.

I'd like to thank my two sons Jalen and Christopher. Jalen thank you for always asking philosophical questions. In my effort to provide a sound answer for you, great insight flowed from me, much of which is written here. Christopher thank you for your support. When I was nervous and scared about where to start you said, "Just start with the Word, Mommy."

Thank you Son.

A special thanks to Michelle and my little darling Kaerah Eva.

I thank my sibs Tammy, Jamie and Jeremy. You know, just for being sibs and supporting me when you didn't even know it. I love you all.

I thank my grandmothers Mull and Big Momma. You both played a role in molding me through my childhood up until your transitions. I think of you two often. And I mustn't leave out the band of important women in my life, my aunties! Yes! I'd also like to thank my adopted aunts in the church and community; Ministers of ODCF past and present; My childhood pastor, Bro. Donnie Williams, and my Sunday School teacher Mrs. Clara Kate.

My host of cousins. Lastly, my students. Many times during lecture, I'd stop mid-sentence and jot things down. It was the contents of this book! I would often have those eureka moments. Thank you all for your stimulating questions. You know who you are.

Thank you.

BIOGRAPHY

Dr. Kristy Cromblin is a mother of two and a new nana of one. She completed her undergraduate studies at the University of Alabama, where she received her BS in Pre-med Biology. She then went on to pursue her dream in medicine. She completed her degree, and joined the ranks of academic medicine. She has over twenty years of medical experience stemming from her years as a medic in the military and onward into her medical profession as a medical doctor. Though she is not active in practice, she aspires to resume her training in the near future.

Childhood. Her mother recalls being in awe at how she would respond with such wisdom at a very young age. Not only does her mother recall her wisdom, but she most recalls her questions. Her mother states that she would never stop asking questions. At times the debates were a bit heated as young Kristy would not settle for certain answers. Therefore, it is not surprising that she ventured on an eleven year journey to find God for herself. She recalls how she stopped taking communion at church because her childhood pastor made a decree that if you were not living right and you took communion, then you were going to burn in hell! Being the literal and gullible young girl that she was, she became terrified at the thought of burning in hell. She stated that because she had a "curse word in her head"

some days prior, she stopped taking communion. She humors at the fact that her parents often times dismissed her regards, as she was well known in the family for being a self-thinker, and plainly put, just way different. Surprisingly, she adds that they never bothered with forcing her to take communion. It took her over a decade to participate in communion again. Dr. Cromblin states that it wasn't that she felt that she was now perfect, but that she had embarked on a journey to know.

Maturing. From her journey to *know*, Dr. Cromblin began to understand God in a less traditional, but more profound way. He unveiled His complexities to her in many ways. She recalls that around the age of fourteen she had an experience that set her on a new path. She began to sense inner wisdom with more keenness. Dr. Cromblin recalls that the inner wisdom would often come around two weeks after she had inquired of something either outwardly or from within. Just a simple, "I wonder why..." She states that when these experiences first began in her teen years they would always be preceded by an impetuous sense of peace and overwhelming euphoria. In fact, of her very first experience she recalls saying out loud, "Wow. This must be what heaven feels like." For over fifteen years she told no one of her experiences, as she states that they were "...too indescribable." She also adds that she was already having to scale back on the image of *overt uniqueness*. She also notes several other spiritual experiences over the years. In time, it became obvious that she was going to have to organize her notes and share them. Speaking engagements and church events became an outlet for much of them. She recalls that in 2012, a minister by the name of Dr. Julian Thomas prophesied to her that the thing that she was working on was going to be an inspiration. Though he was not aware of what it was, she then knew that she had a major task ahead. However, Dr. Cromblin admits that she was slothful and just plain out hesitant about organizing her notes, harboring the erroneous notion that they were *hers* and not to be openly shared. Over the years she began to see much of the wisdom that God had given her was becoming mainstream and common knowledge. She knew that if she was going to actually move forward with the undertaking she had to do so soon, as she didn't want the information in the book to be stale knowledge. She often times thought of a statement that her Uncle Larry would repeatedly make, *"The Lord's work gon' be done, one way or another. The Lord's work gon' be done!"* It certainly rang true when she thought of it in this context. She knew right away that it was no longer about her. Recalling the parable of the man who kept his talents to himself and buried them in the ground, she could not sit still on this mission much longer. Yet it took her some time thereafter. In January 2018, Dr. Cromblin became determined to compile her notes and realize her goal. Personally, I am glad that she did. Reading her notes has come with unforeseen revelation in my own life.

Dr. Hoang Nguyen, PharmD, MD, PhD, FCP
Assistant Professor of Pharmacology CDU/UCLA
School of Medicine and Health Sciences

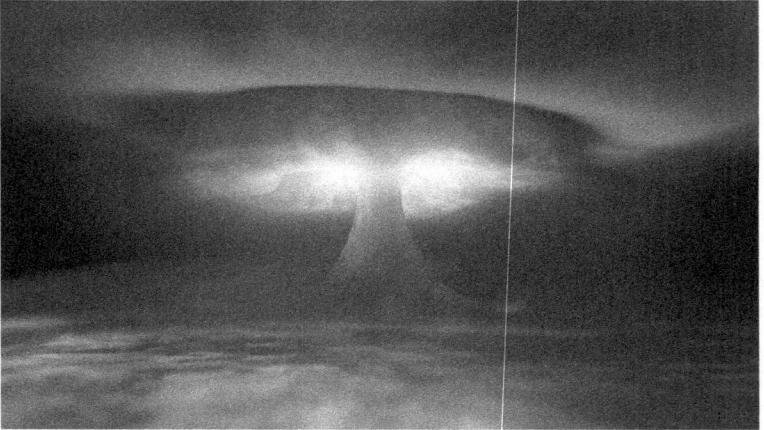

HEATED AIR RISES!
One Prayer. One Sound.

Join us weekly as we concentrate our attention on worldly happenings at:

https://www.kristycromblin.com

NOTES

Schedule your personal coaching session now through
December 2019 at: https://www.kristycromblin.com

NOTES

Comment on my blog at https://www.kristycromblin.com

© 2018 *Made in His Image* is a Life Expectancy, LLC project.

https://www.kristycromblin.com

ISBN 978-0-692-19732-5

9 780692 197325

90000>

www.ingramcontent.com/pod-product-compliance
Lightning Source LLC
Chambersburg PA
CBHW051828040426
42447CB00006B/416